"Boys are alike the world over. They are by nature free from the prejudices and suspicions of their fathers."

ROBERT BADEN-POWELL

From the portrait by David Jagger

Robert Baden-Powell, Chief Scout of the World

Scouting
with
Baden-Powell

RUSSELL FREEDMAN

Holiday House, Inc.   New York

The author wishes to express his gratitude to the staff of Baden-Powell House, London, for assistance in gathering research material for this book; to the British Boy Scouts Association for furnishing photographs from its files and drawings by Baden-Powell; and to Robert Miner of the Boy Scouts of America Editorial Service for reading and commenting on the manuscript. Any errors of fact or interpretation are, of course, the author's responsibility.

Quotations from Baden-Powell's books, articles, and speeches appear with the permission of the Boy Scouts Association. Acknowledgment also is made to Oxford University Press, London, for permission to quote from *Baden-Powell* by E.E. Reynolds.

All drawings unless otherwise noted are by Robert Baden-Powell.

Contents

CONTENTS

The Two Lives of
Robert Baden-Powell

CREEPING, PAUSING, then creeping again, the man moved cautiously up the hill through the darkness. He kept his head low and his shoulders hunched, and he leaned forward slightly, like an animal poised to attack.

Suddenly his foot nudged a loose stone. It rolled down the hill, making a thin, grating noise.

He froze.

For a few anxious minutes he crouched motionless on the hillside, watching and listening, suspicious of every rock and bush. Finally he crept forward again.

As he neared the crest of the hill he lowered himself to the ground, crawled on his hands and knees, and then stopped. He waited, pressing his slight, wiry frame against the grass. There was a chill in the air. A dull light was beginning to fill the African sky and the stars were fading.

Soon a spark and a glimmer appeared on another hillside across the way, and a fire flared up. Now he could see several Matabele warriors moving about, silhouetted against the glow

7

as they prepared their morning meal. He took a map from the pocket of his khaki shirt and marked the enemy position.

The Matabele knew him. For he would appear in their hills by night and by day, in the most unlikely places, when they least expected him. Then he would disappear mysteriously back into the hills. The Matabele called him "Impeesa" —"The Wolf Who Never Sleeps." They had spread word to capture him alive.

His friends called him "B-P." Back home in England, the public knew him as Lieutenant-Colonel Robert Baden-Powell, cavalry officer and army scout.

Several years passed. One afternoon Robert Baden-Powell moved cautiously along a trail leading through a pine forest, creeping, pausing, then creeping again.

Suddenly he heard a twig snap and branches rustle. He pressed himself against a tree, his arms tight at his sides. A voice shouted, "There he is! Let's get him!"

He dived into the forest, slipping and sliding over pine needles, twisting and turning through the trees. Then he felt something glance off his shoulder. Without looking back, he kept running.

Two more tennis balls hit him. He groaned and slumped to the ground. Five boys raced up, breathless. He opened his eyes and grinned at them.

The game was called "Deer Stalking." Baden-Powell was the deer and the boys were the hunters. It was one of many games the boys played that memorable summer on a small island off the coast of England, where Baden-Powell was holding the world's first Boy Scout camp.

He was now a lieutenant general and a national hero, famous

for his exploits as a war scout. Yet he was about to leave the British Army and devote himself to a new idea—an idea he called "peace-scouting."

Peace-scouting was a unique program for boys based on Baden-Powell's army adventures and on his own boyhood experiences. This program, he felt, would appeal strongly to boys and help them become better citizens and happier men. Nothing like it had ever been attempted.

After spending more than thirty years as a soldier, Baden-Powell gave up his army commission. For the next thirty years he dedicated himself to the world-wide Scout movement he had almost single-handedly created.

"I have had the luck to lead two distinct lives," he once said, "both linked by the common bond of scouting, and both intensely happy."

This is the story of both his lives.

PART ONE

War Scout

1

The Boy Stephe

"I HAVE SUGGESTED scouting as a good thing for boys because I began it myself when I was a boy," Robert Baden-Powell once said. He had never forgotten those wonderful summers when he and his brothers had packed their knapsacks and set out for the open country. They might be called the first scout patrol:

"In the holidays we used to walk through countries like Wales and Scotland, each of us carrying a bag on his back and sleeping out at night wherever we happened to be. Generally we would call at a farm and buy some milk, eggs, butter, and bread, and ask leave to sleep in the hayloft if it was bad weather. Otherwise, in summer time it was very nice to sleep in the open alongside a hedge or haystack, using hay or straw or old newspapers as blankets if it was cold.

"In this way we got around a lot of splendid country where we could see all sorts of animals and birds and strange flowers and plants, which we noted in our log. And we had to make our way by the map we carried, and at night we used to find our way in the dark by using different sets of stars as our guide."

His family called him "Stephe," but his full name was Robert Stephenson Smyth Baden-Powell. Robert Stephenson was his godfather, the famous engineer and bridge builder. Smyth was his mother's maiden name. He barely remembered his father, the Reverend Professor Baden Powell.

Stephe's father had been a distinguished clergyman, a scientist noted for his experiments with heat and light, and a professor of geometry at Oxford University. In 1847 he had married Henrietta Grace Smyth, the daughter of Admiral William Henry Smyth. They had ten children, but only six—Warington, George, Frank, Stephe, Agnes, and Baden—lived past early childhood.

Stephe was born on February 22, 1857. Three years later his father died. Warington, the eldest child, was thirteen. Baden, the youngest, was just a few weeks old.

Professor Powell had left only a small inheritance, but his widow was determined that her children would continue to have all the advantages they had enjoyed while their father was alive. By managing carefully, and with the help of the many Powells and Smyths, Mrs. Powell was able to maintain a big house across the road from Hyde Park, in a fashionable section of London. And she made certain that her sons received scholarships at good boarding schools, so they could enroll at Oxford, prepare for suitable professions, and be a credit to their father. In his honor, she soon changed the family name from Powell to Baden-Powell.

When Stephe was growing up in London during the 1860's,

Baden-Powell's father   *Baden-Powell's mother in 1863*

gentlemen still wore tail-coats, ladies' skirts brushed the ground, and a young boy was expected to answer questions with a "Yes, sir" or a "No, ma'am." Every morning, vendors passed the Baden-Powell house at Number 1, Hyde Park Gate, pushing their barrows and crying out their wares. In the evening the lamplighter appeared with his long torch to ignite the gaslights that lined the street.

On fine days, nannies in white uniforms pushed baby prams along the footpaths in Hyde Park, boys raced by rolling big hoops, and girls walked primly hand-in-hand, for in those Victorian times a girl was not allowed to run or even to hurry. And there were horses everywhere, prancing and snorting down riding paths in the park, or clip-clopping along cobblestone roads, their harnesses jingling as they pulled swift hansom cabs, elegant broughams, and rumbling old omnibuses and delivery vans.

London in the third decade of Queen Victoria s reign was the wealthiest of cities, the capital of a powerful British Empire that embraced colonies, possessions, and protectorates in every part of the world. But in the London of the 1860's there

was also shocking poverty, and a large part of the city's popu-
lation lived in sprawling, squalid slums.

These slums were a long way from Hyde Park Gate, but
Stephe knew about them. His mother devoted part of her time
to "good works" in the poor sections of London, and she had
helped establish a charity hospital and a free day school for
girls. Stephe himself had watched wretched old rag-pickers
shamble through his neighborhood, and he had seen youngsters his own age working as chimney sweeps or as delivery
boys on butcher carts and grocery vans. He understood that
boys like himself belonged to the "higher" classes, while others
belonged to the "lower" classes. People knew their "places"
and it was difficult for any boy, however able and energetic, to
rise above his class.

Stephe also understood that he had certain obligations as
well as privileges. He was expected to observe a strict code of
honor and duty, lead a useful life, and show concern for those
less fortunate than he.

Like his brothers before him, Stephe received his first lessons
at home from his mother and a governess. His father had often
taken the older boys on nature walks through the park and
nearby countryside. When Stephe was still quite young—too
young to go along on camping trips—his older brothers took
him on the same kind of nature walks, talking to him about
plants and animals, and encouraging him to ask questions.

He made good use of this early training at St. John's Lodge,
his grandfather's country home near Aylesbury, Buckingham-
shire. St. John's Lodge was a wonderful place for a boy. Stephe
could run wildly over the hills if he wanted to, and he could
follow rabbit tracks through the woods, search for sparrows'
nests in trees, and coax squirrels out of the bushes with acorns.

Stephe at seven, with Warrington, Frank, Agnes, and Baden.

He could swim in his grandfather's pond during the summer and skate on it in winter. And he could saddle up one of the ponies in the stable and go trotting along shady country lanes or galloping breathlessly across open fields and over hedgerows.

His grandfather, Admiral Smyth, had sailed the world over as an officer in Her Majesty's Navy. He had fought against the French during the Napoleonic Wars and had spent years charting the Mediterranean, earning the nickname "Mediterranean Smyth." Now that he had retired to the country he loved to recall his past adventures, and he often told Stephe about his narrow escapes at sea and his exploits in China and India, Africa and the West Indies.

When Stephe was eleven he left home to attend the Rose Hill School at Tunbridge Wells, not far from London. At the time, England did not yet have a good system of free public education. What were called "public schools" were actually private boarding schools—places such as Eton, Harrow, and Rugby. If a boy expected to enroll at a university, he usually went first to one of these expensive public schools.

Rose Hill was a small place where younger boys prepared to enter the traditional public schools. Stephe spent two years there. His mother, meanwhile, was busy writing letters to the governors and trustees of several public schools, asking a scholarship for him. She was still managing on the modest legacy her husband had left, and the best public schools charged high fees. With the help of friends, and her own gifts of persuasion, she had already obtained scholarships for Warington, George, and Frank. Now it was Stephe's turn.

When he was thirteen he was granted a scholarship as a Gownboy Foundationer at Charterhouse, one of the oldest public schools in England.

2

Charterhouse Days

CHARTERHOUSE WAS IN the heart of London, and when Stephe went there in 1870, it was already five centuries old. It had been built in 1371 as a monastery for Carthusian monks, who spent their days praying and meditating. When King Henry VIII broke with the Church and confiscated all the monasteries in England, Charterhouse became the property of the Crown. Then it passed into private hands, and in 1611, when Shakespeare was alive, the monastery's sombre stone buildings and quiet courtyards were bought by Thomas Sutton, a rich merchant who had lost his family and who wanted to put his fortune to some good use.

In his will, Thomas Sutton set up a Foundation. He asked that Charterhouse be used as a home for elderly men, and as a free school for forty "poore boys of gentle birth." Because of the colorful academic gowns they wore, these "poore boys" became known as Gownboy Foundationers.

Stephe Baden-Powell had received one of these scholarships. A classmate described him at this time as "a boy of medium size, curly red hair, decidedly freckled, with a pair of twinkling eyes that soon won friends for him."

When a new boy entered Charterhouse, he was given two weeks' grace. Then he was assigned to an upper classman and was required to act as his "upper's" uncomplaining servant. This old tradition was observed by many English public schools, and most uppers demanded absolute obedience.

Every morning at seven a porter rang his bell in the doorway of Stephe's dormitory. The boys scrambled out of bed, pulled on their clothes, and began the usual morning rush to get their uppers on the way in time for 8 A.M. classes.

Carrying a jug of steaming hot water, Stephe would hurry down a corridor already crowded with boys rushing back and forth. He would knock on his upper's door, slip inside, nudge the sleeping older boy, announce the time, fill a basin with hot water, light the fireplace, then hopefully announce the time again. His upper would groan, pull the covers over his head, or perhaps reach for a slipper and fling it in Stephe's direction.

That was only expected. Whistling softly, Stephe would race out to fetch tea and toast. If he was lucky, his upper would be washing by the time he got back. But if the older boy was in a bad temper that morning, Stephe would hear that the wash water was too hot or too cool, that the tea was too weak or too strong, that the fire was smoking or the toast burnt, and that he was a blasted idiot.

He was also supposed to run errands, polish shoes, press clothes, and do whatever else he was told. Some new boys rebelled against this bossing and bullying, but the system was enforced by older students and schoolmasters alike, and rebels only made themselves miserable. Stephe had no trouble. His older brothers also expected a certain amount of obedience, and he was used to taking orders from them. He made up his mind to serve his upper cheerfully and look forward to the day when he would be an upper classman.

Stephe did fairly well in his studies at first and began to join various clubs and societies. He had taken piano lessons at home and had learned to play other instruments by ear. Now he signed up as a bugler in the cadet corps, a flugel player in the brass band, and a violinist in the orchestra. To round things out, he sang in the school choir.

Two of his talents won the special admiration of his classmates: he was a talented mimic and a gifted artist. He had been drawing and painting since early childhood, and he could sketch equally well with either his right or left hand. By the time he went to Charterhouse he was accomplished enough to draw excellent caricatures and portraits. In the Common Room during the evening rest period he would show off a little while drawing a boy's portrait by switching his pencil back and forth from one hand to the other.

At home he had learned to imitate the sounds of animals. At Charterhouse he began to imitate his classmates and masters. His favorite subject was Monsieur Buisson, the French master. Standing before his friends in the Common Room, Stephe would shrug his shoulders, turn up his palms, twist his mouth, assume an expression of wounded hopelessness, and exclaim, "Ah, Badden-Povvell! It is in vain—it is not of use!"

From the moment Stephe entered Charterhouse, he began hearing about the students' feud with the butcher boys of Smithfield Market, just outside the school walls. This feud had been going on as long as anyone could remember. One afternoon, while Stephe was watching some older students play soccer, he saw the butcher boys in action for the first time.

A gang of shouting butcher boys suddenly climbed the wall alongside the soccer field and began hurling stones and brickbats at the players. The players returned the fire and tried to advance toward the wall. Years later, Baden-Powell recalled that battle:

"With four or five other boys too small to take part in the actual fray, I was looking on at the battle when we suddenly found the headmaster [Dr. Haig Brown] alongside us, anxiously watching the progress of the fight. He remarked to us:

" 'I think if you boys went through that door in the side wall you might attack the cads in the flank.'

" 'Yes, sir,' one of us replied, 'but the door is locked.'

"The worthy doctor fumbled in his gown and said: 'That is so, but here is the key': and he sent us on our way rejoicing, and our attack was a complete success."

Smithfield boys

A few minutes later an enraged man stormed into the school grounds. He confronted Dr. Haig Brown and complained that while he had been riding past the school on top of an omnibus, a flying stone had nearly knocked out one of his eyes.

"The Doctor expressed his regret," wrote Baden-Powell, "but assured the man he was very lucky not to have lost both his eyes if he was so careless of his safety as to ride on an omnibus when a battle was going on between the boys of Charterhouse and the butcher lads of Smithfield."

The Charterhouse boys and the Smithfield lads were like rival gangs, and Stephe naturally rallied to the support of his own gang. When the butcher boys tried to invade the school grounds, he helped drive them off, and he joked about their Cockney accents with his classmates. Even so, he did not fail to notice the disturbing contrasts between his classmates and the butcher boys.

All Charterhouse students, including the Gownboy Foundationers, came from "good families." They would attend universities, enter professions, and take their places as leaders of Great Britain. The Smithfield boys were the same age, but they had no such expectations. Instead of going to school, they worked long hours at the market, and instead of wearing colorful academic gowns, they wore bloodstained aprons. Their wild manners, their unkempt appearance, and their common speech set them in a class apart. Their world was confined to the brawling, congested slums around Smithfield Market.

Baden-Powell remembered the Smithfield butcher boys years later, when he first thought of starting the Boy Scouts. But as a thirteen-year-old student at Charterhouse, he knew only that they were on one side of the school wall while he was on the other.

On school holidays, Stephe and his brothers would go hiking and camping in the country. Warington, George, and Frank were all students at Oxford by now. Before going to Oxford, Warington had served as a midshipman in the merchant service, and while he had finally decided to become an attorney instead of a naval officer, he never lost his love of sailing. One year he designed and built a little collapsible canvas boat that was just big enough to carry three passengers.

Stephe was fifteen when he, Warington and George set out from London in Warington's boat on a remarkable inland trip. Although there is no river leading from London to Wales, the brothers were heading for Wales, where they were to meet the rest of the family. They paddled northward up the River Thames through the peaceful English countryside, carrying tents and cooking gear and camping out at night along the shore. They caught fish, hunted birds and rabbits, and bought the rest of the food they needed at villages and farms along the way:

"We went up the Thames as far as we could go, until the river became a stream and finally a brook that was too small to float us. Then we carried our boat over the hills and got it afloat in another stream running the other way. This stream grew bigger and bigger until it became the River Avon."

They sailed down the Avon until it emptied into the mouth of the mighty River Severn. Then they rowed across the mouth of the Severn, seven miles wide at this point, and when they reached the other side they began to paddle up still another river, the Wye, which led northward into Wales.

When they reached Wales and announced that they had sailed all the way from London, people laughed. Any fool knew that you couldn't go from London to Wales in a little canvas boat.

The summer of the collapsible boat trip was the same summer that Charterhouse moved to larger and more modern quarters near the town of Godalming, Surrey, about thirty-five miles from London. The new school stood atop a broad hill overlooking the fertile valley of the River Wey.

Stephe helped organize a boating club and rifle corps. He joined the debating team and began to contribute drawings and articles to the school magazine, *The Carthusian*. And he played cricket, soccer, and hockey. Games were important at Charterhouse, but he was not a very skillful athlete. He decided to concentrate on one game, soccer, and by practicing hard enough he won a reputation as "a good goalkeeper, always keeping very cool."

The activities he enjoyed most were amateur theatricals. Since he could act, sing, do imitations, play several musical instruments, and paint posters and scenery, he was always in demand.

Once, when a scheduled performer failed to appear at a school variety show, Dr. Haig Brown asked Stephe to fill in by improvising a skit. "Fortunately, the French master was not present," the headmaster recalled, "for he described a lesson in French with perfect mimicry. It was inimitable. It kept the boys in perfect roars of laughter."

Stephe also joined a secret society called the Druids Club. The Druids took their name not from the Celtic priests of ancient Britain, but from the president of their club, W.W. Drew. Each member had a special nickname—Captain Perrywinkle, Mr. Pecksniff Sniffles, Mr. Slug, Mr. Long, Professor Sheepskin, and so forth. Young Baden-Powell was called Lord Bathing-Towel.

At their Saturday night meetings, the Druids drank enormous quantities of ginger beer, told improvised stories, made up songs, and sang old favorites such as "Hearts of Oak" and "Keel Row." Sometimes they held cricket matches with another secret society, the Maniacs.

The Druids Club Minutes Book still exists, its pages decorated with outrageous drawings by Lord Bathing-Towel. It sets forth these rules:

1. Any brother not producing a song or speech within a minute after being called on, the latter in length not less than five minutes, shall be fined a bottle of lemonade.

2. Any brother refusing to pay a fine shall have to pay double.

3. No bad puns allowed, except led by a string, or on exceptional business.

4. Any brother interrupting another brother while singing, must sing two songs himself.

While Stephe enjoyed belonging to clubs, playing games, and performing on stage before an audience, there was another side to his life at Charterhouse. Often he felt the need to go off by himself. He would slip away from the school grounds and disappear into the Copse, a stretch of wild woodland on the hillside below the school's playing fields.

Since the Copse was out-of-bounds, he learned to avoid the masters who sometimes patroled it. "It was here," he wrote later, "that I used to imagine myself a backwoodsman, trapper and Scout. I used to creep about warily looking for 'sign' and getting 'close-up' observations of rabbits, squirrels, rats and birds. . . .

Hiding in the Copse

"I also gained sufficient cunning to hide up in trees when danger threatened, since experience told me that masters hunting for boys seldom looked upward. . . .

"Thus, without knowing it, I was gaining an education that was to be of infinite value to me later."

By moving silently through the woods and then "freezing" in order to watch a bird, a squirrel or a butterfly, he became "a comrade instead of an interloper in the family of nature." He said later that his secret excursions to the Copse were more important to him than the lessons he learned in class or on the playing fields.

With all these activities, he didn't have much time left over for his schoolwork. "I was not a clever boy," he later wrote, "nor, I grieve to say, was I as industrious a boy as I ought to have been. According to my school reports I began fairly well in my work but deteriorated as I went on."

Here are some of his school reports:

Classics: "Seems to me to take very little interest in his work."

French: "Could do well, but has become very lazy; often sleeps in school."

Natural Science: "Pays not the slightest attention."

Mathematics: "Has to all intents and purposes given up the study of mathematics."

Stephe soon found himself in the headmaster's office. Fortunately, Dr. Haig Brown was an unusual headmaster and he didn't care much for rigid rules or harsh discipline. He allowed his boys a great deal of freedom, for he felt that each boy should have a chance to follow his own bent.

While Stephe was neither a brilliant scholar nor an outstanding athlete, Dr. Haig Brown recognized that he possessed some unusual qualities. He was a gifted actor and artist, and a skillful debater. He had a quick sense of humor, and if he was lazy in class, he was certainly energetic outside the classroom.

Even so, academic work could not be shirked and Dr. Haig Brown warned Stephe that if he did not show real improvement, he could not expect to graduate. The headmaster also wrote to Mrs. Baden-Powell, assuring her that Stephe's ability was "greater than would appear by the results of his work."

He did improve. By the time he reached Form VI, the top class at Charterhouse, his Classics master was able to report: "Satisfactory in every respect."

Stephe's three older brothers had saved enough money to buy a small yacht, the *Diamond,* and they began to spend their holidays sailing in the English Channel. Baden, the youngest brother, had now joined Stephe at Charterhouse,

Stephe at seventeen—at Charterhouse

and the two of them went along, too. Since Warington was the eldest and had served in the merchant service, he was of course the ship's captain.

"We younger boys picked up our knowledge from him," Stephe wrote later, "and from our own mistakes. We learned not only navigation and boat-handling, but all about bending the sails, rigging and painting the ship, deck-scrubbing, cleaning, and carpentry. Also, of course, we had to be able to cook and—most important of all, perhaps—to swim."

The brothers soon exchanged the *Diamond* for a larger boat, the *Kohinoor,* which was built to Warington's own design. With the *Kohinoor* they were able to take more ambitious voyages: "We had the time of our lives, cruising around the coasts of Scotland and England at all seasons of the year. Many a scrape—in both senses of the word—we got into and got out of, and thereby gained a lot of useful experiences."

Stephe graduated from Charterhouse in 1876, when he was nineteen. He hadn't decided on a career yet, but he expected to enroll at Oxford, like his father and brothers before him.

He applied for admission to two of the residential colleges at Oxford—Balliol and Christ Church—and took his entrance exams. But while his work at Charterhouse had improved, it hadn't improved enough.

"The author of *Alice in Wonderland* [Professor Charles Dodgson, better known as Lewis Carroll] was my examiner in mathematics," he wrote later, "and he found out what I could already have told him, but what I hoped he would not discover for himself, that it was a subject about which I knew little or nothing. I had a vague hope that my father's reputation as Professor of Geometry might carry me through that gate to the University. But my hopes were vain."

Both colleges turned him down.

3

The 13th Hussars

STEPHE RETURNED TO London to face his mother. At first, she thought he was joking. Failed? How could a Baden-Powell fail his Oxford exams? Stephe's father had earned a brilliant reputation at Oxford. Warington had recently received his law degree there. George had just won the Chancellor's Prize at Balliol College, and Frank was attending Balliol on a scholarship.

But Stephe had failed.

A few weeks later he saw a newspaper announcement that seemed to offer a way out of his troubles. Competitive examinations for officers' commissions in Her Majesty's Army would be held that summer in London.

Candidates had to be between the ages of seventeen and twenty. A "preliminary examination" would be followed by a "further examination" in any four of the following: mathematics, English composition, Latin, Greek, French, German, experimental science, and geography. A fifth exam in freehand drawing was required of all candidates.

Stephe studied the list. Free-hand drawing would be easy for him. He would do well in English composition, and if he studied, he could pass geography without difficulty. That left two choices. Math was out of the question, and so was French. Experimental science was a possibility. And then Latin perhaps.

He tried to imagine himself as an army officer, but he had never even considered a military career before. There was no military tradition on his father's side of the family; the Powells had always been merchants and landowners, clergymen, professors, and attorneys. On his mother's side, however, Grandfather Smyth had been an admiral and Uncle Henry Smyth was now an army colonel. Both men had reached high ranks, and both had traveled widely.

A life of travel . . . if he won a commission he might go anywhere in the Empire—to Africa or India, the Far East or the West Indies. He would have a chance to roam the world and know those same distant lands his grandfather had talked so much about. He could look forward to a life of adventure and challenge, the kind of life he had read about in books. Besides, he had to make a decision about his future.

He decided to take the exams. Since the same set of exams

counted for either the Infantry or the Cavalry, he signed up for both. Then he took his schoolbooks down from the shelf. There wasn't much time. He would have to spend every minute cramming.

The army exams were held at London University between July 3 and July 17. When they were over, Stephe went sailing on the *Kohinoor* and waited for the results to be announced.

One morning he and his brothers were cruising near the Isle of Wight when they passed the *Gertrude,* a yacht belonging to Professor Alfred Acland, a family friend. The professor hailed the brothers and invited them aboard. Among his guests was Dean Henry Liddell of Christ Church College at Oxford, one of the colleges that had rejected Stephe.

"The Dean accosted me," Stephe recalled, "with the news that, according to his morning newspaper, a namesake of mine had passed his exams for the Army. I looked, and there, in black and white, was my own name!"

Stephe's name appeared near the top of the list. Of 718 candidates who had taken the exams, he had placed fifth for the Infantry and second for the Cavalry.

When Mrs. Baden-Powell heard the news, she was jubilant. She had known all along that Oxford had misjudged her son. There was still one problem, however. Most young men who sought army commissions during the 1870's were independently wealthy. Officers had heavy personal expenses and it was considered impossible for a junior officer to live on his pay. As a sub-lieutenant, Stephe would earn only ten pounds a month.

The Baden-Powells held a family conference. Everyone agreed that Stephe should accept his commission. The family would help support him at first—just as they would have supported him at Oxford. Although the Cavalry involved higher

Baden-Powell as a young lieutenant in the 13th Hussars

expenses than the Infantry, it was the more glamorous branch and the one Stephe preferred. His mother insisted that he take the Cavalry commission, and that closed the matter.

Before long a letter arrived addressed to Sub-lieutenant R.S.S. Baden-Powell. Stephe had been assigned to the 13th Hussars, a famous old cavalry regiment with a proud history. The 13th had fought in the Napoleonic Wars and had taken part in the Charge of the Light Brigade, during the Crimean War. Now the regiment was stationed at Lucknow, in the north of India.

Stephe was to sail for India aboard the troopship *Serapis,* leaving Portsmouth Harbor on October 30, 1876.

Like most ocean-going ships of her day, the *Serapis* was equipped with both steam-engines and a full set of sails. More than a thousand officers, soldiers, wives, and children were aboard when she steamed out of Portsmouth at the beginning of her five-week voyage to India.

Baden-Powell described the voyage years later in a book called *Indian Memories*. "My quarters," he wrote, "were in a kind of den below the water-line along the keel of the ship and close to the rudder and screw. It was called 'Pandemonium' because it was a deep, dark, underground place, and from want of ventilation almost as stuffy and hot as its namesake. Here we were jammed together in small compartments holding three or four apiece; but it was so unpleasant that the merciful authorities allowed us to sleep on the stairs or in the passages, wherever we liked, in fact. Often during the night we would be roused by the ship's officers and master-at-arms, going their rounds, to inquire why we were sleeping there. If the answer was 'Pandemonium,' the reason was considered sufficient and nothing further was said."

Stephe kept a diary during the voyage, wrote long letters home, sketched scenes aboard ship, and studied Hindustani, one of the chief languages of India. He also acted and sang in theatricals which were presented on an outdoor stage on the poop deck, and he helped paint the scenery.

The *Serapis* sailed southward through the Bay of Biscay and along the Spanish and Portuguese coasts. On November 8 they passed Gibraltar and entered the Mediterranean.

When the ship called at Valetta, the capital of Malta, Stephe went ashore to visit the Governor's Palace and an old Capuchin monastery. At Port Said, Egypt, they stopped again to take on coal. Then they entered the Suez Canal, completed just seven years earlier. "It is a dreary scene," Stephe wrote, "low banks of mud, beyond them on one side a sandy desert, and on the other a lagoon stretching away to the horizon."

A brisk wind was blowing as the *Serapis* sailed out into the

Arabian Sea. The ship's sails were unfurled and she skimmed swiftly over the waves, heading toward the coast of India. She entered Bombay Harbor on the morning of December 6, and all the officers aboard celebrated their arrival by parading on deck in full-dress uniform.

During the voyage Stephe had made friends with Tommy Dimond, another young sub-lieutenant who also was reporting to the 13th Hussars. "I can well remember," he wrote later, "the trouble my companion and I had in getting our baggage safely ashore, loaded on to a bullock-wagon, and conveyed from the docks to Watson's Hotel. We had donned our best uniforms and were not a little proud of ourselves in the early part of the day; but as hour followed hour in that soggy heat we seemed to melt into the thick tight-bound cloth, and we wished we had something more seasonable to wear. By night-fall we were dog tired and our pride had all leaked out, and under the cover of darkness we willingly climbed up onto the pile of luggage on our bullock-cart and allowed ourselves to be ignominiously carried through the back streets of Bombay to the great hotel."

Early the next morning they loaded their baggage on another bullock-cart, made their way through the teeming Bombay streets again, and boarded a train crowded with British government officials and army officers, with rich young Englishmen on their travels, with turbaned merchants dealing in cotton, indigo, and spices, and with fat Brahmans, tall Sikhs from the Punjab, austere Parsees, and bearded Afghans, all wearing strange costumes and speaking stranger tongues.

Finally the train pulled out of the station and started off on its three-day journey across India.

Lucknow was not the noble walled city Stephe had imag-

Entering Bombay

ined. It consisted mainly of dusty roads, lined by mud huts and stunted trees, and crowded with ox-carts and people and wandering cows—roads that stretched for miles along the River Gumti under the hot Indian sun. Every so often several roads opened onto a bazaar shaded by awnings and canopies and noisy with bargaining merchants, gossiping women, shouting children, bleating goats, and cackling hens.

The British garrison was five miles outside Lucknow. When Stephe Baden-Powell and Tommy Dimond reported to their regiment, they were assigned to an officers' bungalow, which they would share, and were issued government ponies. Then they were interviewed by Lieutenant Christie, the regimental adjutant.

Stephe expected Lieutenant Christie to ask how well he could ride a horse and handle a gun. Instead, the lieutenant inquired, "Can you act, sing, or paint scenery?"

At Lucknow, a soldier's talents as an entertainer were just as valued as his military skills. The most pressing problems facing the British Army in India were not war or insurrection; they were boredom and low morale. The weather was often hot and muggy, and there wasn't much for the men to do when they were off duty. As a result, it was all too easy for them to become depressed and lose interest in their work. To help keep up the men's spirits, most regiments put on frequent entertainments.

Lieutenant Christie was delighted to learn that Sub-lieutenant Baden-Powell could act, sing, and paint scenery. Stephe also announced that he could do imitations, perform skits, play musical instruments, design posters, and build sets. He was put to work right away, painting the scenery for a regimental musical.

Meanwhile, he began a strenuous course in basic military training. Along with Tommy Dimond he endured an endless succession of inspections, reviews, and parades. Together, they shared the early miseries of riding school, elementary drill, carbine practice, and sword exercises. Stephe fired his rifle until his shoulder was black-and-blue; he shouted practice commands until his throat was sore; he rode his government pony until he could scarcely sit down for meals.

One of the main pleasures of life for a young cavalry officer in India was polo. Polo players were not allowed to use government ponies, however. They had to buy and maintain their own polo ponies. Since most officers had comfortable private incomes, they could easily afford entire strings of horses. Stephe couldn't afford one horse.

At first he tried to save money by cutting down on his expenses in the officers' mess. He gave up smoking, drank soda water instead of wine, and refused all extras, such as fancy desserts. Before long he was able to write home that he had the lowest mess bill of any officer in the regiment.

Even so, he found it impossible to save enough money to buy a trained polo pony. So he did the next best thing. He bought an ordinary work pony from a local Indian. This Indian earned his living by cutting grass and selling it to British officers as horse fodder. The pony Stephe bought had carried the grass. He didn't have to pay much for the animal, and when he brought him back to the post, he named him Hercules.

"Hercules had to carry the load of grass every day to the market," he wrote, "and the load was as big as himself. That was how he got the name of Hercules. He was the first pony I ever owned, so I ought to have been proud of him. So I was, but he *was* ugly! My word, he was ugly! A little, thin, red chestnut pony, with a head like a fiddle and hip bones sticking up like hat pegs—a miserable-looking rat of a thing."

Hercules

Stephe and Hercules learned to play polo together. "While I learned to hit the ball as we galloped along, Hercules learned that it was his business to take me wherever the ball was going as fast as he possibly could. So he got to be quite quick at seeing the ball and at turning to follow it, and very often his sharp eyes would find it through a cloud of dust before I saw it myself, and away he would go, carrying me to it."

Beginning with Hercules, Stephe managed to build up a whole string of polo ponies. He continued to buy untrained ponies and train them himself. Afterwards he could sell them to other officers at a nice profit.

By the summer of 1877, Stephe had passed his preliminary exams in horsemanship, marksmanship, swordsmanship, and elementary drill. That autumn he began the special eight-month garrison course that would qualify him for promotion to full lieutenant.

The garrison course covered subjects ranging from military law to combat tactics. Stephe found much of this information interesting and worthwhile, yet the classroom lectures dragged on day after day, week after week, and sometimes he drew pictures instead of taking notes. For his own amusement he drew caricatures of his fellow students, his instructors, and officers in his regiment. He even drew some of the Commanding General at Lucknow.

One day he was unexpectedly summoned to the General's office. "He invited me into his sanctum," Stephe wrote later, "and there produced a portfolio of, as it seemed to me, all the scraps and sketches I had ever drawn. He explained that the orderly whose duty it was to sweep up the lecture room had orders always to save any pictures and to bring them to him for his collection. Although people had laughed at my caricatures, no one laughed more heartily than the General himself, but he warned me that caricaturing was not always a safe game to play, and, acting on his advice, I have seldom indulged in it since. For I know that most people, however large-minded they may be, are very liable to be hurt by even harmless little exaggerations of their failings."

The garrison course ended in June, and by then the hot weather had set in. Temperatures climbed to 116 degrees in the shade. Stephe found it impossible to study for his exams during the mid-day heat and he began to stay up half the night. Just before his exams, he came down with a severe fever, but despite it, he took the exams on schedule and passed with a "First Class" rating. He was promoted to lieutenant and was granted a month's leave.

He headed north for the cool mountain air of Simla, a popular resort in the foothills of the Himalayas, high above the steaming Indian plains. In Simla he felt fine, but when he returned south to Lucknow, he again fell ill. It was one of the worst summers in years; the muggy heat continued for weeks without relief, and though Stephe dosed himself with medicine, watched his diet, and got plenty of rest, he could not shake off his persistent fevers.

"During my first year in India," he wrote, "It seemed to me that I was being plugged full of medicine almost every day. . . . I became so wretchedly thin that I had to have my pantaloons taken in and I could put three fingers between my legs and my top boots, which once were quite tight."

The weather finally turned cool in October, but Stephe's condition grew worse. In November the regimental doctor ordered him to the hospital. There he was examined by other doctors who found he was suffering from a long list of ailments brought on by the unaccustomed food and climate of India.

He needed a complete change. The doctors recommended that he be sent back to England on sick leave.

4

Becoming a Scout

MRS. BADEN-POWELL GASPED when her son walked down the gangplank in Southampton. What had the Army done to him? He was pale and gaunt, he had dark circles under his eyes, his dress uniform hung on his bony frame like a limp sack.

The ailing young soldier was taken in hand by his mother and his sister Agnes, and with plenty of rest, hearty English food, and loving care, he soon felt fit again. He was able to spend most of his long leave visiting friends, catching up on the latest shows at London's theatres and music-halls, and sailing with his brothers on the *Kohinoor*. Warington had managed to combine his love of the sea with his profession as an attorney, for he was now an Admiralty barrister. Frank was also an attorney, and George was an official in the Colonial Office. Baden was just finishing up at Charterhouse; he had decided to follow Stephe into the Army.

That summer Stephe's leave was extended so he could attend the Army's School of Musketry near London. The year-long course would enable him to become a small arms instructor, with a welcome increase in pay, when he rejoined his regiment.

He completed the course in the autumn of 1880, again earning a First Class certificate, and sailed back to India aboard
the troopship *Serapis*. But when he reached Lucknow, the
13th Hussars were gone. They had left a few days earlier for
the remote mountain kingdom of Afghanistan.

Afghanistan occupied a strategic position between Russia
and British India. For decades, Russia and Britain had both
attempted to dominate the mountain kingdom, and their
power struggle had resulted in the Afghan Wars. The latest
conflict had broken out while Stephe was in England. After a
celebrated three-hundred-mile march led by General Sir F.S.
Roberts, British troops had defeated an Afghan army near the
walled city of Kandahar and were now occupying Afghanistan
until a new government, friendly to Britain, could assume
power.

The 13th Hussars had been ordered north to join the British occupation forces at Kandahar. A few men had stayed
behind in Lucknow, under command of a sergeant-major.
Stephe's orders were to leave Lucknow immediately and try to
catch up with the rest of the regiment.

"That day," he wrote later, "a new regimental doctor arrived at Lucknow, and as I was the only officer there, he reported to me. He was accompanied by a lad apparently about
fourteen. After some conversation, he agreed to join me in my
journey to overtake the regiment. I asked: 'What will you do
with your son?'

" 'My son? This is not my son. This is an officer who has
come to join the 13th.' "

The officer was Lieutenant Kenneth McLaren, "who on account of his appearance was fated ever afterwards to be called
'The Boy.' "

Baden-Powell, McLaren, and the doctor boarded a train in Lucknow. With their horses riding in the baggage car, they traveled north to the Punjab and then west into the desolate mountains and deserts of Baluchistan on India's northwest frontier. Their train finally reached the Baluchi town of Sibi, the main British supply base for Afghanistan.

"The train simply stopped in the middle of the desert," Baden-Powell wrote, "among a heap of baggage, bales of clothing, thousands of ponies, camels, mules, and millions of flies. We pitched our tent and had rations served out to us, just the same as to the men.

"The next day we went on to the end of the temporary [railway] line at the foot of the mountain. Here the railway ended, no station or anything; we simply got out of the train, saddled our horses, and rode to camp a little way off, where transport ponies were supplied. We slept the night there in a shed, then packed our things onto the ponies, ourselves onto our horses, and started our march early in the morning."

Their destination was Quetta, the mountain capital of Baluchistan, where they hoped to catch up with the 13th Hussars. For the next eight days Baden-Powell, McLaren, and the doctor rode their horses and led their transport ponies northward through rugged mountain gorges and across stretches of open desert. But when they reached Quetta, the 13th had already left.

Here they joined a dozen other British soldiers, including several men from the 13th who had fallen ill on the march north and had stayed behind in Quetta to rest. The worst part of the journey was still ahead. Now they had to travel across the Kojak, a rugged mountain range separating British Baluchistan from Afghanistan. Hostile Afghan tribesmen were roaming these mountains on horseback:

"After Quetta we were not allowed to travel alone, as that was the enemy's country, and every party was accompanied by an escort of native cavalry. . . . At the first camp we stopped at, some friendly natives came in all covered with wounds they had just got from some Afghans, and we passed another wounded man on the road. We were told that in going up the road, the 13th had found the bodies of three men with their hands tied and their throats cut."

They advanced over the mountains with their revolvers at the ready. "We had eleven bullock-carts, five ponies and mules, and twelve camels. The steep rough road was a tremendous strain on all the animals, especially the camels, when the road was at all wet. Their feet seem to slip in all directions and they were very apt to split themselves by their legs sliding apart. The consequence was dead camels on either side of the road all the way along.

"We would never have made it over the pass had we not met with a company of native infantry and a lot of friendly Afghans, whom we set to work to haul up the carts. When we were over, going down the other side was just as bad, the road being terribly steep and zigzagging down the precipice. The carts had ropes behind with men hanging on to prevent them from running away downhill and going over the cliff instead of turning at the corners. We got into camp long after dark in a storm of sleet."

At last they rode into the Afghan city of Kandahar, "a wonderfully interesting place, but not quite so large as I had expected." It was a city of flat-roofed houses and narrow alleyways, surrounded by huge gray walls pockmarked with bullet holes left by the recent fighting. Outside the main gate stood a rough gallows, the execution site for Afghan rebels and bandits.

The 13th was stationed at a little village called Kokoran, about seven miles outside Kandahar. Baden-Powell was put in command of a mounted troop and was ordered to patrol the surrounding area, draw maps, and report on the activities of local tribes. During that winter of 1880-81, he went out on his first actual scouting and reconnaissance missions.

Mounted on a black charger, a rifle across his back and pistols at his sides, he would lead his men over windswept mountain passes and through silent ravines. It was dangerous work, for the mountains were infested with bandits waiting to ambush supply caravans coming in from India, and with Afghan rebels, superb horsemen who wore knives in their belts and long white robes which flew wildly in the wind. Despite the dangers—or perhaps because of them—Stephe came to love these scouting missions. For when he rode into enemy territory with his little band of men, watching for tracks, listening for suspicious sounds, alert to the slightest movement in the distance, he felt more alive and aware than ever before.

Sometimes he and his men were assigned to night sentry duty. They would leave Kokoran at dusk, set up camp about a mile away, and send out hourly patrols all night long. "It was the best possible form of military training for us youngsters,"

Afghanistan:
Sentry on night duty

he wrote. "It taught us by actual practice in the field rather than through the tedium of barrack-square instruction. . . . We succeeded in getting a great deal of experience, as we were constantly expecting attacks, and the long and bitterly cold nights on outpost duty hardened us thoroughly."

It was a terrible winter—heavy snows, sudden blizzards, and torrential downpours of rain and sleet which flooded the British campsites and swept away tents. Many soldiers died of exposure or disease, or were killed by Afghan rebels and bandits. "We of the 13th were lucky," Baden-Powell wrote, "losing only one man up there through pneumonia. The 11th lost an average of one man a day all the time they were there, and all the other regiments also lost large numbers."

During the winter Stephe was asked by Colonel Baker Russell, his regimental commander, to organize some entertainment for the men. He called for volunteers, had a stage built in the mess hall, and worked out a program of comic songs and skits.

The show was a great success, and similar shows were held every Saturday night at Kokoran. One Saturday night, when several high-ranking officers from India were in the area on an inspection tour, a dignified major-general with gray hair and mustache unexpectedly entered the mess hall auditorium.

Colonel Russell barked a command and the audience snapped to attention. The Colonel welcomed the General to the regimental concert and offered him a seat in the front row.

"No, thank you," the General replied. "Not at all. I've come to help entertain the men. Sit down, men! Sit down!"

As the audience gaped, the General mounted the stage and broke into a hearty rendition of the Major-General's song from the Gilbert and Sullivan operetta, *The Pirates of Penzance.*

Some of the men suspected that the visiting General was an imposter, but they weren't sure and they were afraid to say anything. They were right. For when the General finished singing, he ripped off his gray hair and mustache and revealed himself as Lieutenant Baden-Powell. He had borrowed a general's uniform from an aide-de-camp who was a friend of his.

That spring a new government took power in Afghanistan and British troops began to withdraw from the country. The 13th Hussars moved south to Quetta, just over the frontier, and stayed there for several months.

Apart from practice maneuvers, there wasn't much to do in Quetta. Stephe continued to organize entertainments for the men. He also wrote some articles about army life in this part of the world, illustrated them with pen-and-ink sketches, and sent them to a London newspaper called the *Graphic*. He had met the editor the year before and they had agreed that the *Graphic* would buy any suitable articles or drawings that Stephe mailed in.

This was the beginning of his career as a talented journalist, author, and illustrator. Ever since his childhood he had tried to express himself by writing, drawing, and painting. Since joining the Army he had kept a diary and had filled many of its pages with sketches and watercolors. The articles he sent to the *Graphic* were based on entries in his diary. Later diaries would furnish material for a great many articles and books about his experiences.

His regiment left Quetta in the autumn of 1881 and moved to a new permanent station near the city of Muttra, in northern India. By now Stephe had become close friends with Kenneth McLaren, known throughout the regiment as "The Boy." In Muttra they shared an officers' bungalow with its own garden and stable. Most of the officers in the 13th called Baden-Powell "B-P," but McLaren called him "The Bloater," and their bungalow was known as "Bloater Park."

Baden-Powell was now appointed adjutant, or special assistant, to Colonel Baker Russell, the regimental commander. Colonel Russell was a striking man, standing well over six feet, with powerful shoulders, a big black mustache, and a booming voice. B-P described him as "The ideal fighting leader. . . . I believe that the officers and men would have followed him anywhere."

As Colonel Russell's adjutant, Baden-Powell learned some valuable lessons about handling men. The Colonel believed that the way to bring out the best in a man was to encourage him to think for himself and act on his own. "He was in no way guided by the drill book," B-P wrote, "and knew little and cared less for the prescribed words of command. . . . He gave responsibility and trusted his officers."

Under Colonel Russell's guidance, Baden-Powell had plenty of opportunity to take on responsibilities. Along with his duties as adjutant, he was appointed small arms instructor and riding instructor for the regiment. Because of his practical scouting experience in Afghanistan, he was also asked to start a scouting and reconnaissance course for non-commissioned officers. He wrote a series of classroom lectures for the course and worked out some practical field exercises.

Meanwhile, he had developed a passion for the dangerous sport of hog hunting, or as it was often called, pigsticking. The animals involved were not ordinary domestic pigs. They were wild Indian boars—ferocious beasts as big as donkeys, armed with sharp, ugly tusks. The Indians hated and feared these boars, since the animals often destroyed crops and sometimes attacked people.

Pigsticking

Pigsticking was rough, risky, and extremely popular among cavalry officers in India. The boars were hunted by parties of three or four officers, mounted on horseback and armed with long bamboo spears. Indian beaters would drive a boar out of his lair in the jungle and the horsemen would give chase, galloping across dusty clearings, splashing through stagnant ponds, twisting and turning through high grass and tangled bush, until one of the men finally speared the animal, or until it escaped. Often an enraged boar would turn on his pursuers, flashing his tusks. Horses were gored. Sometimes men were killed.

B-P became an expert at the sport and in 1883 entered the famous pigsticking tournament held in the Kadir Jungle near Meerut. He won the Kadir Cup, the most highly prized pigsticking trophy in India. "Yes, hog hunting is a brutal sport," he wrote later, "and yet I loved it, as I also loved the fine old fellow I fought against."

That same year, when he was twenty-six, Baden-Powell was promoted to captain. At about this time he began to write an army manual based on the scouting and reconnaissance course he was teaching. When the manuscript was finished, he sent it to his brother George in London. George found a publisher and the little manual, called *Reconnaissance and Scouting,* came out in 1884. It was Baden-Powell's first published book.

In November, 1884, after spending three years at Muttra, the 13th was ordered back to England for home duty. The regiment traveled to Bombay by train, then boarded the troopship *Serapis.*

Once they had sailed, however, word spread through the ship that they were not going to England after all. The *Serapis* had changed course. They were heading for the British colony of Natal, in South Africa.

5

Scouting in South Africa

THE 13TH HUSSARS landed at Durban, the chief seaport of Natal, and marched through the streets to the British garrison just outside town. Their orders were to stand by in case of war between British and Boer settlers in South Africa.

"Boer" comes from a Dutch word meaning "farmer." The Boers were descendants of Dutch farmers who began settling in South Africa during the late 1600's. They were followed by British settlers, and as the rival groups competed for fertile land and for control of the region's rich gold and diamond mines, angry disputes started to break out.

By the mid-1800's, Britain had established two crown colonies in South Africa—Cape Colony on the southern coast and Natal on the eastern coast. Many Boers, dissatisfied with British rule, left these coastal areas and moved into the interior. They set up two independent republics—the Orange Free

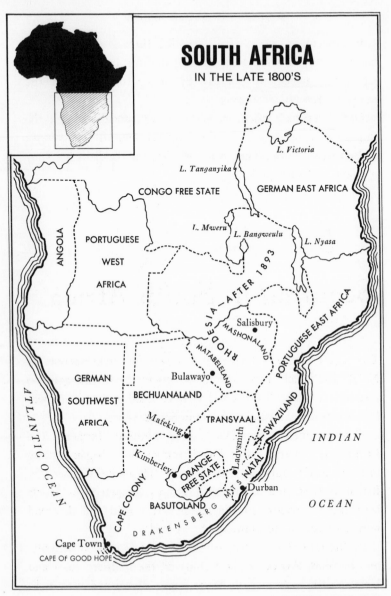

SOUTH AFRICA
IN THE LATE 1800'S

L. Victoria

L. Tanganyika

CONGO FREE STATE

GERMAN EAST AFRICA

ANGOLA

PORTUGUESE

WEST

AFRICA

L. Mweru

L. Bangweulu

L. Nyasa

RHODESIA — AFTER 1893

MASHONALAND

Salisbury

PORTUGUESE EAST AFRICA

MATABELELAND

GERMAN

SOUTHWEST

AFRICA

BECHUANALAND

Bulawayo

SWAZILAND

Mafeking

TRANSVAAL

ATLANTIC OCEAN

Kimberley

ORANGE
FREE STATE

Ladysmith

NATAL

INDIAN

CAPE COLONY

Durban

BASUTOLAND

MTS

OCEAN

DRAKENSBERG

Cape Town

CAPE OF GOOD HOPE

Map by Gilbert Etheredge

State south of the River Vaal, and the Transvaal north of that river.

The disputes between the British and the Boers continued, however, and grew steadily more bitter. The latest dispute concerned the vast region of Bechuanaland, which lay west of the Transvaal and north of Cape Colony and was inhabited mainly by African tribes. Many Boer settlers were beginning to move into Bechuanaland, and the British feared that the Transvaal government might attempt to take over the region.

As a precaution, a British army of four thousand men entered Bechuanaland and moved into positions near the Transvaal frontier. British reinforcements, including Baden-Powell's regiment, were ordered to stand by in Cape Colony and Natal. Meanwhile, British and Boer negotiators were trying to reach a peaceful settlement.

In Natal, the 13th Hussars drilled, paraded, and waited. If war came, Colonel Baker Russell was to lead his men across the rugged Drakensberg Mountains, which marked the frontier between Natal and the two Boer republics. The main mountain passes would be heavily guarded by the Boers during a war. There were other little-known passes over the mountains, however, and Colonel Russell needed accurate information about them. He ordered his adjutant, Captain Baden-Powell, to go into the Drakensbergs and get that information.

B-P's scouting experience and his skills as an artist made him the ideal man to survey this mountain region and draw maps and sketches. His acting ability would help too, for he would have to carry out his mission in absolute secrecy. He decided to pose as a newspaper correspondent collecting material for a series of articles about settlers in South Africa. This disguise

Spying in Drakensberg mountains

would explain why he was wandering about, asking questions, taking notes, and drawing maps.

He grew a scraggly red beard, bought some second-hand civilian clothing, then disappeared into the mountains, riding one horse and leading another that carried his tent, blankets, and rations. For the next month he rode back and forth through the Drakensbergs, sketching and surveying, living on army rations, sleeping at night in open fields or at friendly farmhouses, and talking to everyone he met—Boer farmers, British traders, Zulu tribesmen. As he went along he corrected existing maps of the region, made new maps of his own, and constantly sought suitable ways to cross the mountains. He covered nearly six hundred miles and gained his first intimate knowledge of the country that was to play such an important part in his life.

When he returned to his regiment, deeply freckled by the sun, his red beard more scraggly than ever, he wrote a detailed report, added the maps he had drawn, and submitted it to Colonel Russell. Soon afterwards, British and Boer negotiators settled their dispute peacefully. Not a shot had been fired. For the time being, there would be no war, no sudden marches across the Drakensbergs.

The 13th Hussars sailed home to England in the autumn of 1885. Captain Baden-Powell was put in command of a regimental detachment stationed first at Colchester, on the east coast of England, and later at Liverpool, on the west coast. He took a course in veterinary medicine, then taught the skills he had learned to his men. And he worked out a unique system of drilling the men by means of silent hand signals instead of shouted commands. With this system, he could move an entire mounted troop forward without speaking a word, an obvious advantage if an enemy was nearby.

He also conducted precision riding drills until his men were able to perform a musical dance on horseback to the accompaniment of the regimental orchestra. While B-P delighted in this accomplishment, it was no mere stunt. Any cavalry troop expert enough to dance to music would acquit itself well on a battlefield.

Home duty wasn't very eventful, however, and B-P was able to spend much of his time with his family in London. During his leaves he traveled to several European countries with his younger brother, Baden, now a lieutenant in the Scots Guards. Yet he soon grew restless. He was anxious to serve overseas again.

The opportunity came from his uncle, Henry Smyth. In December, 1887, General Smyth was named Commander-in-Chief of British forces in South Africa, and he asked Baden-Powell to go along as his aide-de-camp. B-P jumped at the offer. He was granted a leave-of-absence from the 13th Hussars, and by the beginning of 1888, he was back in South Africa.

But life as his uncle's aide-de-camp was just as routine as home duty had been. General Smyth's headquarters were in Capetown, the capital of Cape Colony and a large, modern city. Baden-Powell kept regular office hours and spent most of his time answering correspondence, reviewing military reports, and making appointments for the General. For excitement, he played polo twice a week, went deer hunting, joined an amateur theatrical group, and attended the endless round of dinners, receptions, and dances given by the British community in Capetown. "It was hardly what one would call soldiering," he complained.

That summer, a violent Zulu uprising gave the thirty-one-year-old captain a chance to do some real soldiering.

The Zulus were proud warriors and cattle-raisers who lived along the east coast of South Africa, mainly within the British colony of Natal. Early in the 1800's they had fought bitterly against Boer settlers moving onto their lands, and later they had fought just as bitterly against the British. These conflicts had led to the great Zulu War of 1878-79, when British forces, after suffering several defeats, finally overpowered a large Zulu army.

After the war, British authorities divided Zululand into thirteen districts. Twelve of these districts were ruled by Zulu chiefs; the thirteenth was ruled by John Dunn, an old Scottish trader who had lived among the Zulus since his boyhood and who had gained their respect and trust.

This division did not bring peace to Zululand, however. Some of the stronger chiefs began to raid districts ruled by rival chiefs, stealing cattle and burning villages. Before long, civil war raged throughout the area. Several hundred heavily armed Boer adventurers took sides in this civil war and helped Chief Dinizulu of the Usutu tribe gain power over neighboring tribes. As their reward, the Boers demanded a large slice of Zulu territory.

Chief Dinizulu

Chief Dinizulu then turned to the British for protection against the Boer demands. Since British officials feared that the Boers would try to take over all of Zululand, they acted quickly. In 1887, Britain annexed Zululand and placed the territory under the administration of the Governor of Natal.

This was not what Dinizulu had expected. With a few other rebel chiefs, he began to attack the Zulus who had declared their loyalty to Britain, and he launched a campaign to drive all European traders and missionaries out of the territory.

In the summer of 1888, the Governor of Natal appealed to Capetown for military aid. General Smyth mustered an army of two thousand British troops and left for Zululand with his aide-de-camp, Captain Baden-Powell.

The General set up headquarters at Eshowe, the only large European settlement in Zululand. His most urgent task was to send help to a fort at the mouth of the River Umfolozi, where Dinizulu and his allies had besieged several hundred loyal Zulus and Europeans. Forty men defending the fort had already been killed.

General Smyth put Major McKean of the 6th Royal Dragoons in command of four hundred mounted British troops and two hundred loyal Zulu police. McKean picked Baden-Powell as his staff officer, and they set off immediately for the besieged fort.

On their second day out of Eshowe they joined forces with an "impi," or army, of two thousand Zulu warriors, led by the old Scottish trader, Chief John Dunn.

"I shall never forget my first meeting with a Zulu army," B-P wrote. "I heard a sound in the distance which at first I thought was an organ playing in Church, and I thought for the moment that we must be approaching a mission station over the brow of the hill. But when we topped the rise we saw moving up towards us from the valley below three long lines of men marching in single file and singing a wonderful anthem as they marched."

The words of the Zulu anthem sounded like this:

"Een-gonyama Gonyama!

"Invooboo! Yah-bo! Yah-bo! Invooboo!"

"Both the sight and the sound were intensely impressive," B-P continued. "And the men themselves looked so splendid. They were as a rule fine, strong, muscular fellows with handsome faces. . . . their brown bodies were polished with oil and looked like bronze statues. Their heads were covered with ostrich plumes and they had swaying kilts of foxes' tails and stripes of fur, while around their knees and elbows were fastened white cows' tails as a sign that they were on the warpath.

"They carried huge shields of ox-hide on the left arm, each regiment having a shield of its own special color, while in the right they carried two or three throwing assegais [spears] for hurling at the enemy, and a broad-bladed stabbing assegai which they kept for hand-to-hand fighting. In their girdles was slung a club or axe for polishing off purposes.

"With four impis of this kind against us, we felt that we were lucky in having at any rate one such force on our side, and under such a man as John Dunn."

John Dunn was at the head of his impi. B-P asked him to translate the Zulu anthem his men had been singing. Dunn laughed and replied: "He is a lion. Yes, he is better than a lion—he is a hippopotamus."

The combined force of British troops, Zulu police, and John Dunn's impi advanced swiftly through rebel territory. Occasionally they caught a glimpse of rebel scouts disappearing into the bush. But when they reached the besieged fort, Dinizulu and his allies were gone.

John Dunn and warrior

Some of the men in the relief force remained at the fort. B-P and the others escorted the women, children, and badly wounded men back to Eshowe. Except for a few elusive enemy scouts, they saw no signs of Dinizulu's warriors.

General Smyth now sent heavily armed columns into rebel territory, hoping to end organized resistance by a show of force. After a few skirmishes, many of the rebels surrendered. But Dinizulu and hundreds of his warriors continued to hide out in the bush.

At this point, General Smyth took advantage of his aide-de-camp's scouting experience. He ordered Baden-Powell to find Dinizulu. B-P recruited a contingent of Zulu scouts, and accompanied by small detachments of British troops, they began to search for the rebel chief.

They soon found that Dinizulu was entrenched atop a forbidding mountain called the Ceza. General Smyth moved his headquarters to within a few miles of the rebel stronghold and prepared to attack. He put Baden-Powell in command of an advance column of British troops and Zulu warriors.

As B-P and his men climbed a ridge leading to the Ceza, they saw several rebel warriors scrambling into the caves of an opposite ridge. B-P's men hit the ground, taking cover behind clumps of bushes and boulders. Bursts of gunfire echoed from the caves across the way, and bullets zinged off rocks and sent up spurts of earth. B-P ordered his men to spread out and attack the rebels from either side. Racing from boulder to boulder, then diving for cover again, firing constantly at the dark enemy caves, the men gradually closed in on the outnumbered rebels. Suddenly the enemy fire ceased and several warriors emerged from the caves with their arms held high above their heads. Four of their comrades had been killed.

That night, B-P led his advance column deeper into the

Dinizulu's stronghold

Ceza bush, to the very foot of Dinizulu's mountain stronghold. At daybreak his men stormed the mountain, racing up its steep slopes across boulders and ravines until they reached the network of small wooden huts and hastily built stone forts at the summit. But most of the huts had been burned. The forts were empty. The mountain was deserted.

During the night, Dinizulu had escaped with his followers across the frontier into the Transvaal Republic. Yet he realized now that further resistance was futile. A few days later he returned to Zululand and surrendered peacefully to British authorities. The rebellion was over.

Baden-Powell returned to the quiet routine of his Capetown

office and spent another year and a half in South Africa. In 1889 he completed a new book, one he had been working on ever since he had left India. Called *Pigsticking or Hoghunting,* and illustrated with B-P's own drawings and water-colors, it became the authoritative work on that once-popular sport.

Early in 1890, General Smyth's tour of duty as Commanding General in South Africa ended. He was assigned to a new post on the island of Malta, a British possession in the Mediterranean, and he took his aide-de-camp along with him.

6

The Adventures of a Spy

MALTA WAS A sunny Mediterranean island and a strategic British naval base and army garrison. General Smyth had been appointed Governor and Commander-in-Chief. With his staff, he moved into the old Governor's Palace in Valetta, the island's seaport capital.

Baden-Powell, newly promoted to major, served as the General's military secretary and senior aide-de-camp. Again, his duties consisted mainly of routine office work. He began to study Italian, spoken by many of Malta's people, he explored the island's ancient ruins and prehistoric caves, and he organized weekly theatricals for the troops of the British garrison. By charging a small admission fee to these shows, he raised enough money to transform an unused hospital in Valetta into a well-equipped Soldiers' and Sailors' Club.

A more exciting assignment came along in the summer of 1890, when the War Office appointed B-P Intelligence Officer for the Mediterranean. His job was to gather information about military installations and troop maneuvers in countries on or near the Mediterranean. During the next three years, while continuing his staff duties on Malta, he left the island many times to go on spying missions. He later described his experiences in a book called *My Adventures as a Spy*.

B-P's acting skill had given him the ability to meet almost any situation by changing his voice, his appearance, and his manner. As an artist he could draw accurate maps and sketches of anything he saw. And as an experienced scout, he knew how to observe carefully and draw logical conclusions from his observations.

In fact, scouting and spying had much in common. "Spying," B-P wrote, "is secretly gaining military information in peacetime in preparation for eventualities. . . . Scouting on the other hand is the gaining of information about an enemy during the ordinary course of military practice."

On his first spying mission he traveled to North Africa—to the seaport of Bizerta in the French protectorate of Tunisia. The French were enlarging the harbor at Bizerta and were building a ship canal leading from the harbor to an inland lake. A few British officials suspected that France might be establishing a new naval base here; but most British officials rejected this idea, since the French already had an important naval base at Toulon, only 250 miles away. B-P's instructions were to find out what the French were doing.

He went to a small hotel and rented a room overlooking the new ship canal and inland lake. For a week or so he roamed about the harbor area, dressed as a snipe hunter. He carried a hunting rifle, of course, and even shot some snipe. But at every opportunity he drew maps and sketches and asked discreet questions.

When he returned to Malta he sent his maps and sketches to the War Office in London, reporting that the probable purpose of the harbor construction was to turn Bizerta into a major naval base. Although he was complimented on his report, most British officials continued to believe that the French were simply improving the harbor. Events later justified B-P's report, however, for within three years the naval base at Bizerta was in operation.

Another spying mission took him to Dalmatia, on the Adriatic Sea. Dalmatia is now part of Yugoslavia, but at that time it belonged to the Austro-Hungarian Empire. B-P's instructions were to investigate the fortifications at Kotor, a Dalmatian seaport and an important Austro-Hungarian naval base. This time he posed as a butterfly collector.

The day after he arrived in Kotor, he climbed the steep hills rising behind the town, taking his butterfly nets and a sketchbook with him. He had already drawn several butterflies in

"The Butterfly Hunter"

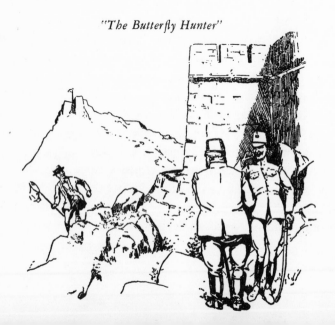

the sketchbook; some of the drawings were complete, but others were only in outline. When he reached the top of the hills, with their sweeping view of the town, the port, the naval base, and the fortifications, he began to make mysterious marks in his sketchbook.

Of course, there were many sentries patroling these hills, but whenever B-P spotted one, he immediately went up to him. "With my sketchbook in hand," he wrote, "I would innocently ask a sentry whether he had seen such-and-such a butterfly in the neighborhood, as I was anxious to catch one. Ninety-nine out of a hundred did not know one butterfly from another—any more than I did—so I was on fairly safe ground. They thoroughly sympathized with the mad Englishman who was hunting insects."

If a sentry asked to see his sketchbook, B-P showed it to him proudly. For the sketchbook contained nothing more than beautiful drawings of butterflies. The sentries didn't realize that some of these drawings were actually clever maps. Carefully disguised marks on the butterflies' wings pinpointed all the fortifications at Kotor, and the position and caliber of every cannon and machine gun visible from the hills.

In Turkey, B-P spied on the defenses of the Dardenelles, the narrow strait that controls navigation between the Mediterranean and the Black Sea. He carried out this mission with the aid of the Scottish Captain of the S.S. *Wallachia,* a tramp steamer carrying grain from a Black Sea port.

B-P boarded the *Wallachia* in Constantinople and stayed with the ship as it steamed slowly through the Dardenelles. "The Captain entered fully into my scheme," he wrote, "and when we arrived opposite any fort in which I had a special interest he would come to anchor, and lower a boat for me to go 'fishing.' "

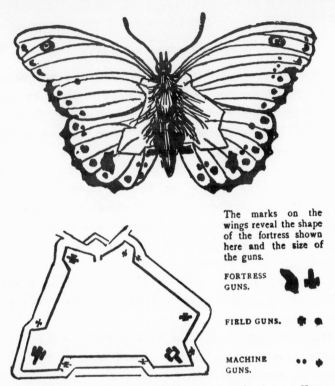

The marks on the wings reveal the shape of the fortress shown here and the size of the guns.

FORTRESS GUNS.

FIELD GUNS.

MACHINE GUNS.

B-P's sketch of a butterfly showing the fortifications at Kotor

Before long a Turkish patrol boat would come speeding alongside to find out why the ship had stopped. As the Turkish officers approached, they would hear the sounds of loud hammering coming from the ship's engine room. The Scottish Captain, shouting above the noise, would tell the officers that the ship's engines had broken down; as soon as they were fixed, the *Wallachia* would be on its way again. Meanwhile, could the officers advise the Captain's "nephew," who was "fishing" in a boat alongside, what kind of bait was best in this area?

B-P was fishing for information, of course. He was taking notes and making sketches of the Turkish forts along the Dardenelles.

"Some of these forts," he wrote, "were reputed to be armed with a brand-new kind of gun about which there was much question. I was able to get to the bottom of this through a friend of mine, a lady who lived in Constantinople and who was on friendly terms with the Turkish Commandant of one of the most important defense works. She persuaded him to invite her to tea in his quarters, and to bring me with her.

"Strolling about the fort after tea I drew attention to one of the mysterious guns covered with canvas sheeting, and he laughingly explained as he lifted the cover: 'These are the same old guns that have been here for years, but we thought it advisable, in view of some moves by a certain neighboring power, to let them suppose that we had rearmed ourselves with something very new and very formidable.' "

One summer B-P turned his attention to Italian army maneuvers in the Alps. He knew the general vicinity of the maneuvers, but he did not know exactly where they were taking place. Posing as an artist, he carried his sketchbooks and water-colors to a small Alpine village where he found a room in an inn. Then he began to wander around, practicing the

The same old guns

Italian he had learned on Malta. Before long, a talkative soldier told him that the maneuvers were being held on the
slopes of a nearby mountain called The Wolf's Tooth.

That night B-P left his inn and headed for the mountain.
By keeping away from regular footpaths, he was able to avoid
the military police patroling the area. He climbed directly
toward The Wolf's Tooth, which he could see silhouetted
against the stars.

"It was a tough and arduous climb, and took me practically
all night, but I got there by dawn, and as I topped the ridge I
saw one of the most astonishingly beautiful sights of my life—
sunrise on a great snow mountain above me. Here I actually
carried out my pretense of being on a sketching tour and made
a rapid water-color drawing of the scene."

As B-P painted, some Italian staff officers appeared suddenly
out of the snow and marched toward him. Since there was no
possible way to escape, he just sat there and kept painting.
When the officers approached, he looked up, smiled pleasantly,
and said, *"Buon giorno."*

Before they could ask any questions, he showed them his
painting. His skill as an artist was so apparent that the officers
immediately accepted his story. They admired the painting,
invited B-P to share their breakfast, and began to tell him all
about the maneuvers that were now getting underway, in full
view on a lower slope of the mountain. B-P pretended not to
be interested, but the less interest he displayed, the more anxious the officers were to explain exactly what was happening.

"They became quite friendly," he wrote, "and showed me
their maps and explained the proceedings, and I spent a day
full of interest watching the ingenious ways in which they got
over the difficulties of mountain climbing with their guns and

mules, and in getting over glaciers and snows with their men roped."

B-P also spied on Austro-Hungarian army maneuvers in the Austrian Alps, on Turkish army maneuvers in Tripoli, and on French army maneuvers in Algeria. Each time he used a different excuse for being in the area, and each time he sent a full report to the War Office in London.

His spying adventures ended in 1893, when he completed his tour of duty on Malta and returned to his regular regiment.

The 13th Hussars were now stationed in Ireland. In the summer of 1893, the regiment took part in the yearly maneuvers of the British Forces in Ireland, commanded by General Sir Garnet Wolseley.

During the maneuvers, B-P's cavalry squadron was instructed to capture an "enemy" gun position atop a small hill. Since the slopes of the hill were bare, it seemed impossible to attack without being sighted by the cavalry troops defending the enemy position.

It hadn't rained for several days, so roads in the area were dusty. Baden-Powell ordered his men to cut the branches off some nearby trees. Then he sent a half-dozen men galloping down a road near the foot of the hill, towing the branches behind them.

Soldiers manning the enemy gun battery saw a great cloud of dust advancing down the road; occasionally a cavalryman was visible through the dust. Only a full squadron could raise so much dust, it seemed, and so the defending cavalry galloped off in pursuit. B-P was waiting with his main force. He attacked the enemy battery from the rear and captured it easily.

A few minutes later, General Wolseley's aide-de-camp came galloping up; Wolseley wanted to see the officer in charge of the attacking squadron. B-P knew that the unusual tactic he had just used would be frowned on by many officers who went strictly by the rule book. "I expected summary dismissal from the Service for playing the fool," he wrote.

When he reported to General Wolseley, the General asked, "Were you responsible for that action?"

"Yes, sir," B-P replied, not daring to look Wolseley in the eye.

The General laughed, clapped B-P on the back, and said, "Now that is exactly the sort of thing I want to see. Use your common sense, sir! Use your common sense!"

General Wolseley was a brilliant career officer, a war hero, and a leading advocate of a more efficient British Army. He was always watching for promising young officers who thought for themselves, men who were willing to put the rule book aside and take chances, even at the risk of making mistakes.

Baden-Powell had come to Wolseley's attention before. The General had reviewed some of the intelligence reports B-P had sent in from the Mediterranean, and he was familiar with the two army training manuals B-P had written, *Reconnaissance and Scouting* and *Cavalry Instruction*. Wolseley knew that the young major had earned an excellent record as a scout in South Africa and Afghanistan, that he had displayed energy and imagination even during the ordinary routine of home duty. In Wolseley's mind, Major Baden-Powell was just the sort of resourceful young officer the modern British Army needed. He remembered B-P.

Two years later, while B-P was still in Ireland with his regiment, he received a telegram from General Wolseley, now Commander-in-Chief of the British Army, ordering him to report to the War Office in London. Wolseley was planning an expedition to Ashanti in West Africa. He had a special assignment for Baden-Powell.

B-P was to join the staff of General Sir Francis Scott, who would command the Ashanti expedition. B-P's special assignment was to raise a contingent of African warriors and scouts who would act as the expedition's advance force.

Just before he sailed for West Africa, he attended a briefing held for all officers going on the expedition. General Wolseley had fought the Ashantis years before, and he warned that they were bold and even reckless adversaries. When they marched into battle, they chanted this war song:

> *If I go forward I die.*
> *If I go backward I die.*
> *Better go forward and die.*

7

The Road to Kumasi

BADEN-POWELL AND the other members of the British expeditionary force arrived aboard the troopship S.S. *Bathurst* at Cape Coast Castle in West Africa on December 13, 1895. Cape Coast Castle was a trading station on the Gold Coast, now part of the country of Ghana, but at that time a British colony. Beyond the Gold Coast, about seventy-five miles inland, lay the vast forest wilderness controlled by the Ashanti Confederacy.

For centuries, Ashanti chiefs had worked with European slavers, raiding peaceful neighboring tribes, killing the children, the old, and the sick, chaining their healthy captives together, and driving them through the forest to trading posts along the coast. The captives were then herded into the holds of waiting ships, which carried them across the Atlantic to the slave plantations of the New World.

This was a profitable business, and the Ashantis grew rich and powerful. They kept many captives as their own slaves, or as victims for the human sacrifices that were part of their religious rites. The Ashanti capital was called Kumasi—a word meaning "the death place."

During the early 1800's, Great Britain and most other European nations finally outlawed the slave trade. But the Ashantis continued to attack neighboring tribes, and now that they had lost their market for slaves, they used more and more of their captives for human sacrifices. Eventually, most of the weaker tribes living near Ashanti territory fled to the safety of the coast, which was under British protection.

When the Ashantis began to raid the coastal region, Britain went to war. Yet the British underestimated both the skill of Ashanti warriors and the perils of malaria and dysentery in West Africa, and at first, British expeditionary forces were overwhelmed by the Ashantis. This situation changed in 1873, when a British army led by Sir Garnet Wolseley marched on the Ashanti capital, captured it, and burned it to the ground.

King Kofi Karikari of the Ashantis then signed the Treaty of Fomena. He agreed to stop all human sacrifices, to remain at peace with his neighbors, to keep a trade road open from Kumasi to the coast, and to pay a war indemnity of fifty thousand ounces of Ashanti gold.

A new Ashanti capital rose from the ashes of the old one,

but the war indemnity was never paid. Later, King Prempeh I repudiated the Treaty of Fomena and the Ashantis resumed their raids and their sacrifices.

When the British decided to send another expeditionary force to Ashanti, General Wolseley knew better than anyone the strength of the Ashantis, the conditions in their country, and the kind of military force needed to defeat them. He placed General Sir Francis Scott in charge of a two-thousand man army. Horses or mules could not be used to carry supplies, because of the deadly tsetse fly and the lack of suitable forage, so twelve thousand African bearers were to be recruited from tribes along the coast. Each soldier would be accompanied by one bearer; the other ten thousand bearers would carry food, ammunition, medicine, telegraph and bridge-building equipment, and other supplies.

Baden-Powell's assignment was to recruit and command a special detachment of African warriors, scouts, and workers. They would go ahead of the main army, clearing a road through the forest, preparing overnight rest camps, and probing into Ashanti territory to determine the enemy's whereabouts and his moves.

B-P went ashore at Cape Coast Castle with his second in command, Captain Graham of the 5th Lancers. During the next few days they recruited five hundred men from friendly tribes living aong the coast. The Mumford tribe furnished workers and bearers; the Krobo and Elmina tribes provided warriors. Chief Andoh of the Elminas agreed to serve as B-P's interpreter, adviser, and guide. He had been General Wolseley's interpreter during the previous Ashanti campaign.

The five hundred recruits reported to the market square in Cape Coast Castle. Baden-Powell and Captain Graham organ-

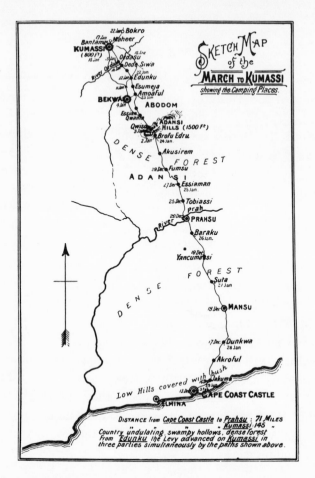

Sketch Map of the MARCH TO KUMASSI showing the Camping Places.

DISTANCE from *Cape Coast Castle* to *Prahsu* : 71 MILES
" " " " *Kumassi*: 145 "
Country undulating, swampy hollows, dense forest
From *Edunku* the Levy advanced on *Kumassi* in
three parties simultaneously by the paths shown above.

ized the men into companies and issued each of them a red fez (a tapered felt hat) with a black tassel hanging from the crown. This would be their only uniform. Some of the men had brought along elephant-hide drums, while others had horns made of hollowed elephant tusks. "At the signal for the march," B-P wrote, "These horns gave out a raucous din, deepened by the rumble of the elephant-hide drums."

Horns blaring, drums rumbling, the advance force marched through the streets of Cape Coast Castle and headed into the interior. They followed the road to Prahsu, a frontier village on the River Prah, about seventy-five miles from Cape Coast Castle. Prahsu was the last British outpost in the Gold Coast colony and the main supply base for the campaign. On the other side of the River Prah lay Ashanti territory.

At first the road was a broad gravel path running across low, bush-covered hills. Then it narrowed and entered a dense tropical forest. This area was under British control, and along the way B-P and his men passed hundreds of African bearers taking supplies to Prahsu. Gangs of workmen were repairing and widening the road, and British engineers were stringing a telegraph line from the coast.

When B-P's men reached Prahsu, they were issued rifles, tools, and food and medical supplies. With the help of his interpreter, Chief Andoh of the Elminas, B-P now recruited 350 more men from tribes living around Prahsu. Among them were one hundred Adansi tribesmen who knew Ashanti territory well and were experts at finding their way through the forest by day or night. These Adansi tribesmen would be B-P's sentries and scouts.

General Scott's main army began arriving in Prahsu a few days later. On December 24, B-P was ordered to cross the River Prah. His men rowed across the sluggish yellow stream in dugout canoes and again plunged into the forest.

"Beyond the Prah," he wrote, "we find a very different state of things. Our road is no longer the comparatively broad, direct and well-cleared way, but has become a twisting, zig-zagging footpath, now clambering over fallen tree-trunks, now twisting through a bog. . . . The thick foliage of the trees, interlaced high overhead, causes a deep, dank gloom, through which the sun seldom penetrates. The path winds among the tree stems and bush, now through mud and morass, now over a steep ascent or a deep ravine. The heavy dews and mists that come

Stringing telegraph wire through Ashanti jungle

at night are laden with malaria for men, while the tsetse fly and horse-sickness infest the forest and bar it as a death trap to all beasts of burden. . . . In all the forest scarce a bird or living thing is seen. An occasional robin's song is heard, or the tuneful wail of the 'finger-glass bird,' while at night the whistle of the crickets and the roar of the frogs is broken by the dismal child-like shriek of the sloth.''

From this point on, B-P's advance party had to clear and widen the trail so it would be passable for the large army following. Slashing through the tangled undergrowth with axes and machetes, B-P and his men moved slowly through the wilderness. They built log roads across swamps, tree-trunk bridges over streams, and earthen ramps across giant fallen trees. Every seven or eight miles they stopped to construct a rest camp for the main army, clearing away the bush and building storehouses for supplies, barricades for defense, and sheds for the men to sleep in:

"On through the deep, dark aisles, still foggy with the morning mist and wet with the dripping dew. Twisting and turning, now up, now down, clambering over giant tree roots or splashing through the sucking mud—all in moist and breathless heat, till, tired and dripping, we reach the next site for camp. Two hours' rest for mid-day chop, and then parade. . . . At last every man has his tool issued to him, and every company has its work assigned to it. . . . The bush comes down. . . . By sunset there is an open space of some seven or eight acres where this morning there was nothing but a sea of jungle. Large palm-thatched sheds have sprung up in regular lines, and in the center stands a nearly finished fort. Within it are two huts, for hospital and storehouse. Trains of carriers are already arriving with hundreds of boxes of beef and biscuit to be checked, arranged and stored."

B-P had noticed Captain R.S. Curtis of the Royal Engineers carrying a heavy, eight-foot wooden staff. The staff was useful for testing swampy ground and jumping across streams, and since it was marked in feet and inches, it could be used to make quick measurements. B-P began to carry a similar staff. He also wore a wide-brimmed Boer hat, similar to an American cowboy hat. The brim protected his face from low branches and vines and shielded his eyes and neck from the hot sun when they reached a clearing. His men began to call him "Kantankye," meaning "He of the Big Hat." Years later, both the wide-brimmed hat and the wooden staff would become part of the first Boy Scout uniform.

During the day, B-P's Adansi scouts probed the forest ahead for signs of the enemy. At night, the watch was kept by parties of a half-dozen men who set up outposts a mile or so beyond the main encampment. "With such outposts," B-P wrote, "our expedition is pretty safe from any surprise by the enemy. Nor is our work confined to passive watching, for far and wide, and well into the enemy's country, our scouts and spies have spread themselves."

As the scouts returned from the reconnaissance missions, they reported that King Prempeh had called his Ashanti chiefs together for a war council, and that thousands of Ashanti warriors were gathering in Kumasi and outlying villages. And yet the advance force came within a few miles of Kumasi without encountering the enemy. Now B-P halted and waited for the main army to catch up. When General Scott arrived, he called his staff officers together to plan the final approach to Kumasi.

Baden-Powell was ordered to send two flanking detachments through the forest; they would enter Kumasi from the west and east. With the rest of his men, he was to advance toward Kumasi along the central trail. The main army would follow a short distance behind.

B-P started off along the central trail. "Warily we went, with scouts creeping and cutting their way through the undergrowth in front and on either side of us. We were now on a regular track leading to the town. Here we found a whole line of little wooden dolls planted in the ground, facing towards the coast. This was a fetish and a gentle hint to us to turn around and go the same way, or otherwise their gods would be exceedingly unkind to us.

"Presently we passed a group of huts, empty at the moment, but evidently of recent occupation: the owners had fled at our coming. Then more huts and openings among the trees, with a high thick jungle of elephant grass all around.

"Suddenly there came a weird sound in the air, the throbbing and boom of drums ahead; some of them far away, some near at hand. The enemy's drums were calling the alarm. . . . Then some of our leading scouts came running back to tell us that we had reached the place. . . .

"Out of the dark, soggy depths of the forest we came, for the first time in weeks, into the open sunshine. There lay before us a clear space like a parade ground, a quarter of a mile wide, and beyond it, on a gentle slope in a hollow, a mass of thatched roofs, stretching away into the jungle beyond."

This was Kumasi, the fabled "death place," but it was not at all what Baden-Powell had expected. Kumasi was "just a vast village, nothing imposing about it; no walls or ramparts, no spires or minarets; yet a place with a long and lurid history of its own; the key to a vast hinterland."

As B-P and his men marched into the clearing, thousands of Ashanti men, women and children thronged from the town to stare. Moments later, B-P's two flanking detachments appeared out of the forest. The drumming had changed now; its tempo was slower. Chief Andoh told B-P that the drums were no longer sounding the alarm. The new drum-talk meant that the Ashantis were willing to "palaver."

Soon the first unit of General Scott's main army marched into the clearing—a company of Gold Coast Haussas, crack African troops led by a drum and fife band. The Haussas formed a line facing the town. Their drums and fifes played on one side of the clearing, while Ashanti drums boomed on the other.

Then the drumming grew louder and the roar of voices filled the air. "Great colored umbrellas were soon seen dancing and bobbing above the heads of the surging crowds of natives as they poured onto the parade ground. Stool-bearers ran before their masters, followed by whirling dancers with their yellow skirts flying around them. Great drums like beer-barrels, decked with human skulls, were booming out their notes, while bands of elephant-tusk horns added to the din. The King and his chiefs were carried into the clearing on elevated chairs and arranged themselves in a dense line along the edge of the parade ground to see the troops arrive. The umbrellas formed a row of booths beneath which the chiefs sat on their brass-nailed chairs, with their courtiers around them. . . . Presently our General and his staff were seen approaching, followed by the main body of troops in military array."

General Scott's army of fourteen thousand soldiers and bearers stretched back along the trail for nearly ten miles. For several hours men streamed out of the forest. As each company reached the clearing, it veered off from the main column and marched away to set up camp.

King Prempeh and his chiefs continued to watch silently from their side of the parade ground. The King, stout and expressionless, sat on a high throne shaded by a huge velvet umbrella. He wore a helmet-shaped crown of black leather, studded with gold ornaments, and strings of gold nuggets around his neck and arms. Three dwarfs, wearing scarlet robes, danced before him. Sword-bearers, heralds, councilors, medicine men, and attendants surrounded him. His tributary chiefs sat on smaller thrones alongside him.

It was late afternoon before the last men of the British force filed out of the forest. General Scott and his aides then sat down on camp-chairs in the middle of the clearing, facing

King Prempeh and his chiefs a short distance away. An interpreter approached the King and asked him to greet the British
commander.

Without a word, the King stood up. Accompanied by attendants, he walked across the clearing. General Scott rose to
meet him. The two men stood facing each other. Finally the
General spoke through his interpreter. He told the King that
the Governor of the Gold Coast was on his way to Kumasi.
When the Governor arrived, King Prempeh must agree to
abide by the twenty-two-year-old Treaty of Fomena.

King Prempeh listened silently. When General Scott had
finished, the King turned, walked back to his throne, sat
down, and was carried back into Kumasi. He had said nothing, he had agreed to nothing.

General Scott's men settled into their campsites and waited.
Guards were posted at every road and bush-path leading out
of town. Baden-Powell was ordered to keep the palace under
surveillance, in case the King or his chiefs attempted to escape.

"A short reconnaissance of the palace," B-P wrote, "showed
it to be a collection of buildings with high-pitched, thatched
roofs in many layers, contained within a high-walled enclo-
sure. A few back-doors in this wall led into a jungle of elephant grass and undergrowth, and beyond this lay a forest."

B-P's men found a secret exit in the palace wall. It opened
onto a hidden footpath through the undergrowth and into the
forest. B-P ordered his men to clear away the undergrowth so
that anyone trying to use the secret exit would have to cross
this cleared area before reaching the forest. Then he posted a
twenty-four hour guard, instructing his sentries to hide in the
trees behind the clearing and wait.

The next two days passed quietly. On January 19, Governor
W.E. Maxwell of the Gold Coast arrived with his escort. A

delegation of British officers informed King Prempeh that he was expected to meet the Governor the next day.

That evening several Ashanti chiefs entered the royal palace, apparently for a conference. B-P was suspicious. He doubled his guard behind the palace and decided to spend the night there himself.

By midnight, a thick mist covered the area. Around 3 A.M., B-P was lying hidden in the elephant grass when he saw a shadowy figure emerge from the secret exit in the palace wall and creep silently across the area that had been cleared two days before. "As soon as he had passed me," B-P wrote, "I gave our little call, the whistle of a frog, 'quit, quit-quit.' This gave warning to the ambushing picket which lay alongside the path a few yards farther on, and as soon as he reached that point he was quietly embraced, gagged, bound, and removed for safekeeping.

"Another and another of these men came at intervals, only to be disposed of in the same way. They were scouts from the palace to see whether the path was clear.

"After a pause, a movement among the shadows showed two men coming very slowly and stealthily one behind the other. Nearer and nearer they came, till at last the leader was close— quite close—in front of me. Here he checked himself, poised and tense, looking forward, trying to pierce the darkness which hid our ambushing party.

"For hours, it seemed, he stood like this, all of us in a state of suspended animation, hardly daring to breathe. . . . Then he turned to whisper to his assistant; he had evidently seen something suspicious. It was time to act. I had only to stand up where I was and reach out to grip him around the neck with one arm, and with my knee in the small of his back to get him down.

Ambush!

"Then we had a rare old rough-and-tumble. . . . we rolled over into the ditch. Fortunately his assistant had sufficient sense of fair play to bolt away, leaving us to have it out between us; and I rather think that my opponent would have had the best of it if it hadn't been that the faithful Musa [B-P's African orderly] slipped in at the exact moment when the Ashanti, having drawn a knife from the back of his belt, was searching for my liver with it.

"All ended well, however. We soon had the man gagged and bound. His assistant had meantime been tripped up and captured by some of my Adansis. After that no more scouts came our way before the day began to dawn."

As the sun rose over Kumasi, everyone began to prepare for the day's big event: the confrontation between Governor Maxwell and King Prempeh. By mid-morning, British troops had assembled on the parade ground before the town and had formed three sides of a huge square. The fourth side was reserved for the King and his retinue. Governor Maxwell and General Scott appeared and sat on a raised platform in the center of the square. The Governor and the General waited.

The British troops stood at rigid attention beneath the glaring tropical sun, and behind the troops, thousands of curious and expectant Ashantis crowded around and milled about.

Then drums and horns sounded, and King Prempeh, the Queen Mother, and the Ashanti chiefs, all sitting on their thrones, were carried onto the parade ground beneath great whirling umbrellas. The townspeople fell back to let the royal procession pass. As soon as the King and his party had taken their places, a fourth line of British troops marched into position behind them.

Governor Maxwell rose and spoke through an interpreter. King Prempeh, he said, must now submit to British authority by honoring the Treaty of Fomena. He must agree to end all human sacrifices and to stop raiding neighboring tribes. He must agree to keep a trade road open to the coast. And finally,

"Palaver" and submission of King Prempeh

he must pay the war indemnity of fifty thousand ounces of Ashanti gold called for by the treaty.

The Governor's speech was brief. When he finished, King Prempeh stood up, took off his crown, and slipped his feet out of his sandals. Barefoot, he approached the raised platform where the Governor was standing. Then he dropped to his knees and embraced the Governor's legs—in the same manner that the chief of a defeated tribe would submit to him.

A shocked murmur rose from the crowd. For centuries the Ashanti Confederacy had been all-powerful. All West Africa knew the saying: "The King of the Ashantis is the lord of heaven and earth." Never before had an Ashanti ruler acted in such a humiliating manner.

"It was a little thing," B-P wrote, "but it was a blow to Ashanti pride and prestige such as they had never suffered before."

If Governor Maxwell was surprised, he gave no sign. Instead, he again told the King that the old war indemnity—fifty thousand ounces of gold—must be paid in full.

King Prempeh replied that such a vast amount of gold was not available in Kumasi. He offered to pay one-twentieth that amount.

The Governor refused. If the full indemnity was not paid immediately, he warned, then the King, the Queen Mother, and the leading chiefs would be deported to Cape Coast Castle.

Governor Maxwell ordered a detachment of British soldiers to search the royal palace and make an inventory of everything they found. They discovered that all the royal treasures had disappeared, including the King's golden hat and his golden chair of state. Apparently, everything had been hidden in the forest before the British arrived. Governor Maxwell now ordered that the King and his chiefs be arrested.

Throughout this entire drama, the townspeople of Kumasi seemed stunned. Baden-Powell believed if they had guessed beforehand what their King would do, they would have fought bitterly to prevent it.

Two days later, the British army began to leave Kumasi. King Prempeh, the Queen Mother, and the chiefs were placed under heavy guard, for there was a rumor that the Ashantis were planning to assassinate the King while he was being escorted back to the coast.

Baden-Powell and his advanced force again went ahead of the main army. This time they searched the forest along the way for signs of any would-be assassins, but there were no incidents of any kind. B-P and his men reached Cape Coast Castle on the morning of January 29, forty-four days after they had first set out on the road to Kumasi.

In the market square, B-P mustered his men for the last time. Chief Andoh interpreted for him as he thanked the men for a job well done, and dismissed them to return to their homes.

"Then, in order to cadge a good breakfast, I went on board the hospital ship *Coromondel*. They gave me a hearty welcome and as I sat in a deck-chair waiting for breakfast, with all my responsibilities off my shoulders, I quietly fell asleep. I did not wake up until the following day to find myself in bed in a comfortable cabin."

The hospital ship was filled with patients. Not a shot had been fired during the Ashanti campaign. Yet more than half the British troops had come down with dysentery or malaria, and dozens of men had died of disease on the road to Kumasi.

King Prempeh and the other members of the royal family were exiled to the Seychelles Islands in the Indian Ocean. The Ashanti Confederacy was dissolved, and five years later, in 1901, Ashanti was declared a British protectorate.

King Prempeh remained in exile until 1924, when he was permitted to return to Kumasi and spend his remaining days among his people. He scarcely recognized his capital, for Kumasi had become a flourishing modern city, linked to the coast by railway. Old King Prempeh had changed too. He became President of the Kumasi Boy Scouts.

When Baden-Powell returned to England, he wrote a vivid account of the Ashanti campaign and illustrated it with his own sketches. Called *The Downfall of Prempeh,* this book was published in 1896 and was dedicated "To Chief Andoh of Elmina, My Guide, Adviser and Friend."

For his services in Ashanti, B-P was promoted, at the age of thirty-nine, to lieutenant colonel. He rejoined the 13th Hussars in Ireland, but he had hardly settled down to regimental life again before he was ordered back to Africa for what he later called "the best adventure of my life."

8

The Wolf Who Never Sleeps

A MONTH AFTER he rejoined his regiment, B-P received urgent orders from the War Office. He had four days to pack his gear and report aboard the troopship S.S. *Tantallon Castle,* sailing May 2, 1896, for Capetown, South Africa. He had been assigned to the staff of General Sir Frederick Carrington, who was already on his way to take charge of operations against rebelling Matabele tribesmen in Rhodesia.

The *Tantallon Castle* reached Capetown on May 19. That same evening B-P boarded a train for the nine-hundred-mile trip to Mafeking, a small town on the northern frontier of Cape Colony, where the railway ended. In Mafeking he caught up with General Carrington and two other members of the General's staff. The next day they all climbed into a stage-coach pulled by eight mules and set off for Bulawayo, six hundred miles farther north and the chief British settlement in Rhodesia.

B-P described this stagecoach as "a regular Buffalo-Bill-Wild-West-Deadwood affair, hung by huge leather straps on a heavy, strongly built under-carriage." General Carrington and his staff officers sat inside. Two drivers rode up front. Three soldier guards rode on the roof with the baggage.

For most of its six hundred miles, the road from Mafeking to Bulawayo was a rutted track stretching as far as the eye could see across flat, arid grassland, dotted with thorn bushes. "It took us ten days and nights to get there," B-P wrote, "the most unrestful journey I have ever endured. . . . Sun baking hot, flies thick as dust. . . . All day and all night we go rocking, pitching and rolling along in the creaking, groaning old coach."

Whenever they came to a wayside mail station, they stopped to change mules. Sometimes they rested for a few hours at a lonely British ranch, marked by a solitary windmill or water-pump, or at a friendly African "kraal," a village surrounded by a protective stockade. All along the road they saw "the grisly, stinking signs of rinderpest," a deadly cattle disease that was sweeping through South Africa.

Coach in Rhodesia

In some areas, the ground was littered with hundreds of dead oxen and mules, and they often passed abandoned coaches and wagons. One afternoon, as their coach bounced along through the dust, one of their own mules stumbled and died.

As they approached Rhodesia they entered the fantastic, moon-like landscape of the Matopo Hills. This was Matabele country, and the guards riding on top of the coach kept their rifles at the ready. The road led through the hills, across the Mangwe Pass, and out onto a grassy plateau. Now they passed small forts, manned by British settlers, every few miles the rest of the way into Bulawayo.

Bulawayo was to be General Carrington's headquarters in his campaign against thousands of Matabele warriors who had sworn to drive the British out of Rhodesia.

The Matabele were descendants of the Zulus. During the 1830's, they had been driven out of their original lands on Africa's southeast coast by rival Zulu tribes and by Boer settlers. They had emigrated to that part of Africa just north of the River Limpopo, had conquered the weaker tribes already living there, and had claimed the region as their new home—Matabeleland.

Matebeleland consisted largely of a great "veld," a Dutch word meaning open grassland with few trees. Much of this veld was excellent for ranching, and the region also abounded in valuable minerals. Until the late 1880's, however, only a few European traders and missionaries had ventured into the region. Then, Matabeleland came to the attention of Cecil Rhodes, the controversial millionaire-politician known throughout Africa as the "Empire Builder."

Rhodes had made an enormous fortune in South Africa's diamond mines. He had then entered politics, becoming first an influential member of the Cape Colony Parliament, and later, Prime Minister and virtual dictator of Cape Colony. This was an era when Great Britain, France, Belgium, Germany, and Portugal were all competing for African colonies. It was Cecil Rhodes's ambition to make all South Africa part of the British Empire.

He was convinced that unless Britain acted, Matabeleland with its riches would be colonized by the South African Boers or by a rival European power. When British authorities refused to take over the territory, as Rhodes had urged, he decided to act on his own.

In 1888 he sent agents north to gain mining concessions from King Lobengula of the Matabele. To exploit these concessions, he then organized a private corporation called the British South Africa Company. Under the sponsorship of this company, miners and ranchers by the thousands began to pour into Matabeleland, and also into neighboring Mashonaland, inhabited by the Mashona tribes, which had long been dominated by the Matabele.

The Matabele King felt that Rhodes had tricked him. Lobengula had been willing to grant mining concessions, but he had not expected so many British settlers to move onto his lands. In 1893 the Matabele tried to drive these settlers out of the region. After a brief war, they were defeated by troops of the British South Africa Company. King Lobengula fled into the bushland to the north, where he soon died of smallpox.

The combined regions of Matabeleland and Mashonaland now became known as Rhodesia and were governed directly by the British South Africa Company. For about three years, British settlers and Matabele tribesmen observed an uneasy truce. Early in 1896, however, Rhodesia was struck by a terrible epidemic of rinderpest, which killed most of the cattle in the territory. Then locusts wiped out much of the grain crop.

As the Matabele watched their cattle die and their grain disappear from the fields, their priests told them that these disasters were punishments inflicted by the gods because they had allowed the white settlers to take over their lands. Once again, the Matabele rebelled. They began to attack outlying mining camps and ranches, killing British settlers wherever they found them. Throughout the territory, settlers fled for safety to the little town of Bulawayo.

The Matabele did not attempt to storm the heavily fortified town. They waited outside and deliberately left the road south open as an escape route, hoping that the British would use this road to get out of the territory. But the settlers did not intend to leave. They meant to stay and fight.

News of the Matabele rebellion traveled south to Capetown and north to the British settlement of Salisbury in Mashonaland. In Salisbury, Cecil Rhodes organized a force of armed settlers and set out for Bulawayo. At the same time, a relief force of British troops rushed northward from Capetown.

In London, the War Office had placed General Carrington in charge of operations against the Matabele rebels. Carrington had asked that Lieutenant-Colonel Baden-Powell be appointed his Chief of Staff.

Carrington's stagecoach arrived in Bulawayo on the morning of June 3, 1896.

Bulawayo was a rough frontier town sprawling some two miles along the road. The market square was barricaded with wagons and sandbags. Just beyond this barricade were barbed-wire entanglements. And beyond the barbed-wire, the ground was covered with a thick sprinkling of broken glass. The entire town was surrounded by electric land mines, which could be set off from a lookout tower on the roof of the market house.

As General Carrington's Chief of Staff, B-P opened an office in Bulawayo and supervised the organization of the British forces. To begin with, the General planned to attack the scattered rebel forces to the north, east and west of Bulawayo. Afterwards, he would send his troops south to the Matopo Hills, where most of the Matabele rebels seemed to be gathering.

According to reports, the Matabele were building fortified kraals throughout the Matopos and were moving into them with their women, their children, and their few remaining cattle. B-P described this region as "awful country, a weird, jumbled mass of gray granite boulders, thickly interspersed with bush, and great jagged mountains. . . . It was the most damnable country that could be imagined for fighting over."

Before sending troops into the Matopos, it would be necessary to reconnoiter the hills, locate the enemy's encampments, and draw maps. General Carrington decided to transfer Baden-Powell's staff duties to another officer; he ordered B-P to spend all his time scouting in the Matopos.

"I needed a really reliable guide and scouting comrade," B-P wrote. "When you are choosing a man for a job like this, where your life is going to depend on him, and, what is also considerably to the point, where he at times will have to rely on you for his life, the selection is not one that can be lightly made."

B-P scouting in the Matopo Hills

He chose Jan Grootboom, a young African of Zulu descent. Grootboom had lived among European settlers for many years, had taken a European name, spoke fluent English, and was an expert hunter and guide. B-P called him "a man of exceptional courage and soldierly ability. . . . a clever scout and a daring spy. I never had to regret my choice. He proved the bravest man I ever saw."

B-P and Grootboom would ride out of Bulawayo at dusk, and as they entered the Matopo Hills, they would dismount and tie their horses' hooves in pieces of blanket, to muffle sound and obscure the tracks. Leading the horses, they would advance cautiously through the gathering darkness into enemy territory. When they were deep in the hills, they would conceal themselves among bush and boulders and wait for dawn.

One morning, just before daylight, they were lying hidden

in the bush on the slope of a hill. "Suddenly on the dark mountainside before us there came a spark and a glimmer and a fire began to burn. Another was lit, another, and then another. The enemy was right there before us, giving away their position."

B-P noticed nothing unusual. But Grootboom turned to him and whispered, "They are laying a trap for us. Wait here and I'll go and see."

Grootboom quickly stripped off his clothing, left it lying in a heap on the ground, and disappeared into the darkness. B-P waited, crouched behind a boulder.

"The worst of spying," he wrote later, "is that it makes you always suspicious, even of your best friends. So as soon as Grootboom was gone in one direction, I crept away in another, taking the horses with me, and got among some rocks on a small rise where I should have some kind of chance if he had any intention of betraying me and bringing the Matabele back to capture me.

"For an hour or more I lay there while the sun rose, until at last I saw Jan crawling back through the grass—alone. Ashamed of my doubts, I crept out to him and found him grinning all over with satisfaction while he was putting on his clothes again."

Grootboom now explained why the Matabele campfires had made him suspicious. Instead of flaring up all over the mountainside at about the same time, the fires had appeared one by one, in regular succession, as if a single man was making the rounds lighting each one.

After leaving B-P, Grootboom had discovered a party of enemy warriors lying in ambush beside the footpath leading to the Matabele encampment. He crept past the warriors without being detected. Then he turned around, stood up, and walked

Matabele warrior

back towards them. Since the Matabele and the Zulus are related and speak the same language, he was able to masquerade as a warrior from a nearby kraal.

"After chatting with them," B-P wrote, "he found out what was their intention with regard to us, and also what were their plans for the near future. When he left them he walked boldly back towards their stronghold, and, once out of their sight, he crept away among the rocks and quietly made his way back to me.

"A job like that carried out in cold blood, with the certainty of death if he failed, demanded a pretty high form of courage. . . . Many and many a time Jan risked his life in similar ways.

When at the end of the campaign I left Matabeleland, we parted as real friends."

The two of them often spent the entire day in enemy territory, seeking out Matabele encampments, estimating the enemy's numbers, drawing sketches and maps. To avoid detection, they wore rubber-soled shoes and clothing that blended with the landscape. The metal on their rifles, pistols, field glasses, wrist watches, and belt buckles was blackened so it would not reflect sunlight. Sometimes they walked backwards for a while, so the Matabele could not follow their tracks. They built campfires in one spot, then moved on somewhere else. And all the while they watched for the smallest signs that might reveal the enemy's whereabouts.

"In scouting," B-P wrote, "the tiniest indications, such as a few grains of displaced sand here, some bent blades of grass there, a leaf foreign to this bit of country, a buck startled from a distant thicket, the impress of raindrop on a spoor, a single flash on the mountainside, a far-off yelp of a dog—all are letters in the page of information you are reading. . . . and that is what goes to make scouting the interesting and absorbing game that it is."

On each of their scouting missions, B-P and Grootboom approached the Matopos from a different direction, explored a different area, and left by a different route. They appeared in the most unexpected places, by day and by night, at dawn and at dusk, as though they never rested, never slept. The Matabele wanted to know how much information these two scouts had gathered, and they spread the word that B-P and Grootboom must be captured alive.

Although Matabele warriors sighted B-P and Grootboom several times, they always managed to escape and disappear back into the hills. "I found out I could, with my rubber-soled shoes, skip away faster than they could follow," B-P wrote. "The ominous call of their chiefs to the runners—'Don't shoot him, catch him with your hands'—was a spur if spur were needed. Just one false step or a twisted ankle would have brought the same result."

The Matabele soon developed a grudging respect for the wiry British soldier and his tall African companion. They began to call B-P "Impeesa," which means "The Wolf Who Never Sleeps."

"Impeesa"—at night

While B-P and Grootboom were prowling through the Matopos, General Carrington's troops were attacking the scattered rebel forces to the north, east and west of Bulawayo. By the middle of July, Carrington was ready to send his men into the Matopos, the center of Matabele resistance.

He placed Colonel Herbert Plumer in charge of operations in the Matopos. Plumer set up camp just south of the hills and began to attack the enemy strongholds one by one.

With Baden-Powell leading the way, Plumer's men would

leave their camp at dusk and set off into the hills. "I preferred to go alone in front of the column," B-P wrote, "for fear of having my attention distracted if anyone were with me, and thereby losing my bearings. There was something of a weird and delightful feeling in mooching along alone, with a dark, silent square of men and horses looming along behind. . . . Except for the occasional cough of a man or snort of a horse, the column, nearly a thousand strong, moved in complete silence.

"First came an advance force comprising two corps of Cape Boys—Africans from Cape Colony, mostly English-speaking, and dressed and armed like Europeans. There were also two hundred friendly Matabele and twenty mounted white scouts. This force was under my direction. Then came the main body of British troops under Colonel Plumer."

When the men came within a mile or so of an enemy kraal, they would stop and rest for a few hours. Just before daybreak they would set out again and approach the Matabele stronghold, which was usually atop a small hill, or kopje. The steep slopes of the kopje were always barricaded with rocks and tree trunks and were often pitted with deep caves. Sometimes the battle over an enemy stronghold lasted several hours. B-P described one such battle:

"We advanced in the growing daylight into the broken, bushy valley, surrounded on all sides by rough, rocky cliffs and kopjes. . . . As you approach the kopjes, excitment seems to be in the air; they stand so still and harmless-looking, and yet you know that from several at least of these caves the enemy are watching you, with a finger on the trigger, waiting for a fair chance. But it is from the least expected quarter that a roar comes forth and a cloud of smoke, and the dust flies up at your feet. . . .

Typical Matabele stronghold

"Suddenly [a Cape Boy] fires into the smoke which spurts from the cave before him. Too late: he falls, and then tries to rise—his leg is shattered. A moment later three of his comrades are around him; they dash past him and disappear into the hole, two dull, thud-like shots within, and presently they come out again . . . then they pick up the injured man by his arms and drag him out into the open, and, leaving him there for the doctor's party to find, they are quickly back again. . . . At one moment they appear on unexpected points of rock, at another creeping around corners and shooting—or being shot. . . ."

Battles like this raged through the Matopos for weeks. The Matabele fought in small groups without any central command, taking full advantage of the natural protection afforded by the hills. Each enemy stronghold had to be attacked separately. Although Colonel Plumer's force was usually outnumbered, his men were equipped with automatic rifles, machine guns and small cannons. Only a few of the Matabele had modern rifles. Most of them were armed with old elephant guns, muskets and blunderbusses, along with their traditional spears and battle-axes.

One by one, the Matabele hilltop fortresses were captured by Colonel Plumer's men. The rebels retreated deeper and deeper into the hills, keeping up a fierce resistance. They had already lost most of their cattle to rinderpest, the British were capturing many of their remaining cattle, and if the war continued, it would be impossible to sow the next season's grain crop. In the end, the Matabele were defeated not by force of arms, but by the threat of starvation.

In mid-August, two Matabele messengers carried a white truce flag into Colonel Plumer's camp and said that the rebels were ready to talk peace. Jan Grootboom helped arrange the talks. Along with two friendly Matabele, he went into the hills, contacted some rebel chiefs, and set the time and place for the first "indaba," or peace conference.

This famous indaba took place on August 22. The British delegation was led by Cecil Rhodes, whom the Matabele called "The Big Brother Who Eats Up Countries for Breakfast." Since the rebel chiefs considered Rhodes the "Chief" of all British settlers in the region, they had insisted on dealing directly with him.

Rhodes was accompanied by two of his assistants, by a newspaper correspondent, and by Jan Grootboom. These five men rode unarmed into the Matopos and dismounted at the agreed-on spot. Rhodes and the others waited while Grootboom disappeared over a nearby hill. He returned leading a procession of forty Matabele "indunas," or chieftains.

Rhodes greeted them in their own language; raising his hand, he said, "Umhlope," the salutation of peace after war. Chief Somabulana, spokesman for the indunas, said that this indaba represented the Matabele nation "as its eyes and ears."

Then everyone sat in a circle on the ground and the conference began.

The peace talks went on for several weeks. Although all fighting in the Matopos had stopped, a few rebel chiefs were still holding out in a district about a hundred miles north of Bulawayo. General Carrington put Baden-Powell in command of a cavalry detachment and ordered him to seek out these rebels.

B-P and his men spent the next six weeks in this remote district, capturing and disarming some of the holdouts and forcing others to flee north into Mashonaland. By the time they returned to Bulawayo, Cecil Rhodes and the Matabele chiefs had signed a peace treaty. The rebellion was over. The Matabele were already beginning to sow their crops, and British settlers were returning to outlying ranches and mining camps. The Matabele had given Rhodes a new name. Now they called him "The Bull Who Separates the Fighting Bulls."

At the beginning of 1897, B-P was back in London, enjoying a two-month's leave with his family. He had just been promoted to full colonel, a high rank for a man of forty. He spent much of his leave working on *The Matabele Campaign,* a book that was read widely in England and has been called one of the finest records of army scouting ever written.

When his leave ended he again returned to his regiment in Ireland. There was now an embarrassing problem, however. B-P outranked his own commanding officer, who was only a lieutenant colonel.

The War Office solved this problem a few weeks later by offering Baden-Powell the command of another cavalry regiment, the 5th Dragoon Guards. The 5th was stationed in India, where he had started his army career twenty-one years earlier.

9
Preparing for War

EACH REGIMENT HAD its own close friendships and proud traditions, and it was never easy for a man to be promoted into another unit. B-P admitted later that he dreaded his first meeting with the officers of the 5th Dragoon Guards. And those officers in turn were waiting to judge the new colonel.

The 5th was part of the large British garrison at Meerut in northern India. B-P had been away from India for years, and he was anxious to try his skill at pigsticking again. Soon after he arrived at Meerut he organized a hunt, knowing that his younger officers would be watching him carefully.

The hunt started off badly, for as the officers gave chase the wild boar escaped into a thick patch of jungle. When Indian beaters failed to find any sign of the animal, B-P dismounted and went to look for himself. He spotted the boar's tracks, but just then the beast came snorting out of the underbrush, head low and tusks flashing.

B-P braced himself and met the attack head-on with the point of his pigsticking lance. The impact knocked him to the ground, but he did not lose his grip. When the other hunters rushed up he was still on his back, holding on to the lance with all his might as the enraged boar struggled to get free. One of the officers quickly killed the animal and then asked, "Do you always hunt on foot, sir?"

B-P staggered to his feet, still dazed. He noticed that all the officers were staring at him in astonished admiration. "On foot?" he replied. "Of course. Why not?"

Any commander who dared stalk a wild boar on foot had little trouble winning the respect of his men. In fact, the 5th Dragoon Guards soon discovered that Colonel Baden-Powell was an unusual commander in many respects.

For one thing, he showed a genuine personal interest in his men's welfare. Since there were few ways for the ordinary soldier to spend his free time at Meerut, B-P opened a pleasant enlisted man's club and introduced a program of frequent sporting events and theatricals. Despite his rank, he was always willing to mount the stage himself and tell jokes, perform skits, or burst into song.

Many officers of the old school considered it undignified for a full colonel to behave in this manner. In their view, a commander should not mingle with the troops; he should remain aloof and stern. These officers ruled according to a harsh code of discipline and often treated their men more as automatons than as human beings.

If the occasion demanded, B-P could be just as impressive as the next officer. But he had never been able to regard men as machines and he knew that a bored, dissatisfied or troubled soldier will not show much enthusiasm for his job. He intended to treat each man in his regiment as a self-respecting individual.

"I am absolutely convinced," he wrote, "that it is the personal touch between the officer and the individual man that commands the stronger discipline—the discipline that comes from within rather than any discipline imposed from without by regulations or fear of punishment."

B-P's training program also emphasized the individual man.

Conventional army training at this time still relied heavily on what one man called "antiquated and useless forms of drill, blind obedience to orders, ramrod-like rigidity on parade, and similar time-honored practices." B-P felt that these practices tended to create unthinking robots. A soldier had to obey orders, of course, but situations often arose when there were no officers around, when an enlisted man had to use his own initiative, trust his own judgment.

This is why Baden-Powell considered scouting and reconnaissance such valuable forms of training. Scouting encouraged a man to be observant and self-reliant, to take on responsibilities, to think for himself instead of always relying on an officer. Besides, scouting was "an absorbing game," as B-P had written. It appealed to the men and challenged them to do their best.

As a young lieutenant in the 13th Hussars, B-P had taught his first course in scouting and reconnaissance. As Commander of the 5th Dragoon Guards he developed a similar course, but now he was able to draw on his varied scouting experiences in Afghanistan, Zululand, Ashanti, and Matabeleland. For this course he worked out a number of games and contests that tested a man's memory, his powers of observation and deduction, and his ability to follow tracks, avoid detection, draw accurate maps, and find his way across unfamiliar territory.

B-P obtained permission to award a special badge to those men who completed the course successfully. It was worn on the right sleeve of the uniform. "I chose the *Fleur-de-lys*," he wrote, "which marks the North point on the compass, as the Scout is the man who can show the way like a compass needle." Since the men had to demonstrate considerable skill before they earned the right to wear this badge, it became a mark of high distinction in the 5th Dragoon Guards.

Years before, B-P had written a small army manual called *Reconnaissance and Scouting.* Now he began to write a new scouting manual, based on the lectures and field exercises he had worked out for his regiment. He planned chapters under such headings as "Finding the Way," "Tracking," "Spying," "Keeping Yourself Hidden," "Sketching," and "Reporting."

Altogether, he spent two years as Commanding Officer of the 5th. In June, 1899, he returned to England on leave, taking the completed manuscript of his new manual, *Aids to Scouting,* with him. This was the book that would later affect the lives of millions of boys.

B-P had expected to return to India at the end of the summer. In July, however, he was summoned to the War Office by the Commander-in-Chief of the British Army. General Wolseley had a new assignment for B-P. He was sending him back to

B-P's army scouts training in India

South Africa, where British and Boer settlers were again on the verge of war.

The political situation in South Africa in 1899 was much the same as it had been fifteen years earlier, when B-P rode through the Drakensberg Mountains on his first important scouting mission. The Dutch Boers still governed two independent republics: the Transvaal and the Orange Free State. Great Britain ruled the prospering crown colonies of Natal and Cape Colony. Directly north of Cape Colony was the vast, sparsely populated territory of Bechuanaland, a British protectorate. And northeast of Bechuanaland was Rhodesia, governed by Cecil Rhodes's British South Africa Company.

Troubles between the British and the Boers had continued despite efforts by both sides to reach peaceful settlements. By the summer of 1899, everyone in South Africa feared war, and many people expected it. The Transvaal and the Orange Free State had formed a military alliance and were buying modern weapons from France and Germany. Great Britain, meanwhile, was sending army reinforcements to the area.

B-P's new assignment was to recruit two mounted infantry regiments in Rhodesia and Bechuanaland. These regiments were to guard the five-hundred-mile frontier separating Rhodesia and Bechuanaland from the Transvaal Republic. If war came, B-P's instructions were to divert as many Boer troops as possible along this frontier and away from the more populous regions farther south.

He sailed immediately for Capetown, then rode the train north to Mafeking, near the Cape Colony-Bechuanaland border. Three years earlier, it had taken him ten days to travel by stagecoach from Mafeking to Bulawayo in Rhodesia. Now the railway extended all the way north to Bulawayo, and he was able to make the trip in less than two days.

In Bulawayo he was joined by a dozen other officers who had been assigned to his staff. One of them was Colonel Herbert Plumer, who had fought with B-P during the Matabele campaign. Another was his old friend Captain Kenneth McLaren, who had served with B-P in India many years before. McLaren was close to forty now, but he was still known as "The Boy."

B-P spent the next two months raising his frontier forces. He recruited one regiment from among British settlers in Rhodesia and placed Colonel Plumer in command; Plumer's headquarters were at Bulawayo. B-P recruited his second regiment from among settlers in Bechuanaland and Cape Colony and put Lieutenant-Colonel C.O. Hore in charge; Hore's headquarters were at Mafeking.

As Commander-in-Chief of the combined force, B-P traveled back and forth between Mafeking and Bulawayo, supervising the recruits' training and seeing that the two regiments were supplied with enough horses, mules, wagons, guns, and ammunition. Meanwhile, British and Boer officials were negotiating in a last attempt to avert war. When the negotiations were broken off in September, B-P decided to move his own headquarters from Bulawayo to Mafeking. Although Mafeking was located in Cape Colony, a few miles below the Bechuanaland border, it was the official capital of Bechuanaland. And while it was just a small, isolated frontier town, it was strategically important.

Mafeking was only eight miles away from the Transvaal frontier—within striking distance of Pretoria, the Transvaal capital. A strong British garrison at Mafeking would force the Boers to divert large numbers of troops in order to protect their own territory.

Mafeking was also a strategic outpost of Cape Colony. If the

Boers wrested control of the town, they could use it as a base to attack the heavily populated regions to the south. A rumor was already spreading that if war came, and if the Boers captured Mafeking, this would be a signal for thousands of Boer settlers living in Cape Colony to rebel against the British.

Finally, as a mid-way point between Cape Colony to the south and Rhodesia to the north, Mafeking was an important transportation center and a depot for large supplies of food, forage and railway equipment that could not be allowed to fall into Boer hands.

Despite its importance, Mafeking wasn't very impressive. B-P called it "a very ordinary looking place. Just a small tin-roofed town of small houses in rectangular streets, plumped down on the open veld." Europeans had settled here only fourteen years before, in 1885, and the railway from Capetown had not arrived until 1894. By 1899, Mafeking boasted a Town Hall and Court House, a bank, a law office, two small hotels, two schools, several churches, a race-course, and a new hospital run by the Irish Sisters of Mercy, who lived in an adjoining convent. Only one building in town was more than a story high. All the buildings had mud-brick walls and corrugated-iron roofs, and during the rainy season, the roofs rattled like thousands of tin drums.

About 1800 people lived in the European section of town. The African quarter, or "stadt," was the home of some 7500 Baralong tribesmen. The River Malopo, muddy and sluggish, flowed through the center of town from east to west. The railway entered from the south, crossed an iron bridge over the Malopo, and ran between the African and European quarters.

And all around, stretching wide and empty to the horizon, was the gently undulating veld, barren and stony, covered with coarse yellow grass and thorn-bushes, broken only by an occasional low hill and by a few scattered gum and acacia trees. These trees were so scarce that the townspeople had given each tree its own name.

Because Mafeking stood on the open veld, it would be a difficult place to defend. The only natural fortification nearby was Cannon Kopje, a hill about two hundred feet high on the southern outskirts of town. Baden-Powell decided to set up an elaborate system of man-made fortifications.

To begin with, work gangs using picks and shovels built a series of sixty small earth and sandbag forts that completely encircled Mafeking, forming a defense perimeter just over five miles around. These forts were linked to each other and to the town itself by a network of trenches. An inner circle of fortified defenses was put up along the edges of town.

For his command headquarters, B-P took over the law office on Market Square, in the center of Mafeking. A wooden lookout tower on the roof of the building provided a clear view of all the outlying defense forts. Alongside the headquarters building was an underground shelter for B-P's staff, its entrance protected by bales of hay. B-P installed a telephone exchange inside this shelter; it was connected to the lookout tower and to each of the outlying forts as well.

Meanwhile, work gangs built a much larger underground shelter nearby for the town's women and children. They dug trenches across Market Square and along every street in Mafeking. And they barricaded all roads leading out of town.

As a final touch, B-P posted notices warning the townspeople that landmines would be buried in the ground just beyond the outlying forts. These mines were made in a secret laboratory run by Major Panzera, an artillery officer. Then

Above ground

Alarm Bell ↑   Bombproof covered with   Traverse of hay
                        Tarpaulin   bales ↑

Below ground

Headquarters office, Mafeking

they were sealed in wooden boxes, carried outside town, and buried with great care. To avoid accidents, a red flag was planted beside each buried mine; if war came, the flags would be removed. Finally, the townspeople were notified that the mines would be tested one afternoon between noon and 2 o'clock. Everyone was warned to stay away from the test area.

Baden-Powell and Major Panzera were the only people in Mafeking who knew that there wasn't nearly enough dynamite in town suitable for these mines. The mines were nothing more than boxes filled with sand.

"With everybody safely indoors," B-P wrote later, "Major Panzera and I went out and stuck a stick of dynamite into an ant-bear hole. We lit a fuse and ran and took cover until the thing went off, which it did with a splendid roar and a vast cloud of dust. Out of the dust emerged a man with a bike who happened to be passing, and he pedaled off as hard as he could go for the Transvaal, eight miles away, where no doubt he told how by merely riding along the road he had hit off a murderous mine."

While B-P was setting up Mafeking's defenses—real and imaginary—he was also mobilizing his forces. The Mafeking garrison included some five hundred officers and men belonging to the Bechuanaland Protectorate Regiment, which B-P had recruited earlier that summer, plus another 250 members of the British South Africa Police, the Cape Police, and the Bechuanaland Rifles, a volunteer army corps. These troops would be responsible for manning the forts outside Mafeking. To man the defenses inside the town, Mayor Whiteley had mustered a Town Guard of three hundred men, a special corps of one hundred railway workers, and several other smaller units. Women volunteered for nursing duty. The Irish Sisters of Mercy set up a casualty ward and operating room at

From a drawing by John H. Bacon

Baden-Powell in his office at Mafeking

their hospital. B-P could count on about 1250 fighting men. His officers were all professional soldiers. The men he had recruited for the Bechuanaland regiment were mostly hard-bitten ranchers, miners and prospectors. The Town Guard was made up of merchants, shopkeepers, clerks, cooks, gardeners, and house-servants. Some of them had never fired a gun.

The majority of these men were British. Some were Dutch Boers who had become British subjects, or who had sided with Britain in this dispute. Others were Swedes, Danes, Germans, Russians, Americans, Indians, Arabians, and Turks. There were sixty "Cape Boys"—Africans from Cape Colony and smaller groups of English-speaking Zulus and other Africans. They had come to this part of South Africa from all over the world and for many different reasons, but they were now united by their common loyalty to Her Majesty's government and their determination to keep the Boers from seizing Mafeking.

The Baralong tribesmen living in Mafeking's African stadt could not be counted as part of the town's garrison. This was a dispute between Great Britain and the Boer republics, and it was understood that if war broke out, neither side would attempt to draw local tribes into the conflict as fighting troops. It was recognized, however, that the Africans had the right to defend themselves and their property. B-P authorized the Baralongs to raise their own special force of armed cattle guards, watchmen, and scouts. The Baralongs in return offered to furnish runners who could carry messages through the Boer lines at night.

On October 9, news came over the telegraph that the Boers had demanded the withdrawal of all British troops from the border areas. Within twenty-four hours, the British government had rejected the ultimatum. On the evening of October 11, the Transvaal and the Orange Free State declared war. When this news reached Mafeking, Baden-Powell declared martial law.

Early the next morning he inspected the three hundred men of the Town Guard, who had assembled in Market Square. "The Boers will never enter Mafeking," he told them. The men cheered wildly and fired their rifles into the air.

Soon afterwards a special evacuation train, carrying nearly two hundred women and children from the European quarter, chugged out of Mafeking and steamed southward across the veld, heading for the town of Kimberley in Cape Colony. About 450 other women and children had chosen to remain in Mafeking with their men. When the evacuation train disappeared over the horizon, groups of people gathered to talk in Market Square, in the lobby of Dixon's Hotel, and on shaded verandahs. Young boys, playing war games, raced through the dusty streets, leaping over sandbags and scrambling into trenches.

On October 13, the telegraph receiver in the railway office stopped clicking. The Boers had cut the wires. Later that day, reconnaissance patrols reported that the Boers had ripped up the railway tracks on both sides of town and were advancing on Mafeking from all directions.

As Baden-Powell stood atop his lookout tower, peering through field glasses, he could see enemy troops streaming across the veld on horseback, in wagons, and on foot. They were coming from the north, east, south, and west. By nightfall, Mafeking was surrounded.

10

Besieged with B-P

THAT EVENING, Baden-Powell summoned his staff officers to a conference. The Boers were moving into four main laagers, or encampments, outside Mafeking. During the night they would probably set up smaller outposts closer to town.

B-P had already decided on the strategy he later called "a

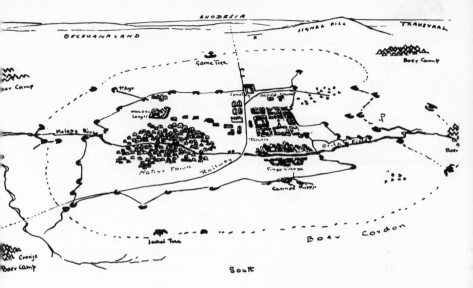

B-P's map of Mafeking besieged

game of bluff from start to finish." His objective was to keep the Boers puzzled, worried and off-guard, to convince them that Mafeking was so strongly defended, so well-equipped, it could never be taken.

His game of bluff had started with the "landmines" buried outside town. The Boers had learned about these mines and for the time being were keeping their distance. B-P's next move was to attack while enemy troops were still moving into their forward outposts.

Earlier that month, Mafeking's railway workers had built two armored trains by walling up freight cars with steel rails and connecting the cars to locomotives. One of these trains had gone south with the women and children evacuees. The other was now used to support Mafeking's surprise attack.

Just before dawn on October 14, B-P sent a mounted patrol led by Captain Charles Bentinck out across the veld with instructions to head north and keep close to the railway tracks. Before long Bentinck's men spotted a faint glow of flickering light—an enemy outpost. The Boers were making their morning coffee.

The patrol dismounted. Two men stayed with the horses while the others crept toward the outpost, advancing close enough to hear Boer voices in the darkness. Bentinck whispered a command. His men hit the ground and fired a single volley.

Several Boer soldiers leaped up in surprise and were silhouetted against their campfire. The patrol fired another volley and the Boers scrambled to take cover behind their wagons. Bentinck's men raced for their horses and galloped off toward the armored train, which was waiting just north of town.

The moment they reached the train, it pulled out for the enemy position. Three machine guns were mounted in the steel-walled cars; seventy men with automatic rifles rode inside the cars or ran along behind. As the train approached the Boer

Armored train

outpost, it screeched to a halt and both sides opened heavy fire.

It was getting light now. The armored train was an easy target but a sturdy fortress. Boer bullets zinged off the steel sides of the train and ricocheted into the dust or whined away across the veld.

There were about four hundred men in the Boer outpost. Twice they attempted to storm the armored train, but both times they were driven back by devastating bursts of machine-gun fire. B-P was watching the battle through field glasses from one of Mafeking's outlying forts, and he decided to send in reinforcements. Fifty more British troops galloped out toward the battle site, dismounted a short distance from the train, left their horses behind a cluster of abandoned native huts, and advanced against the enemy's flank. Caught in the cross-fire, the Boers began to fall back toward their main laager, a mile or so to the rear.

By now, reinforcements from the Boer laager were coming across the veld and were spreading out in an attempt to surround the armored train. At this point, B-P called his men back. The attack had served its purpose; he could not afford to dispatch more men from his small reserves. The armored train withdrew, covered by bursts of machine-gun and rifle fire, and the Boers did not attempt to follow. They had suffered severe casualties in this unexpected skirmish.

Gradually the firing died down. Then it ceased altogether. Boer ambulance wagons, flying Red Cross flags, lumbered out onto the veld to pick up their dead and wounded.

For the next two days, scarcely a shot was fired. The Boers were tightening their cordon around Mafeking, but they did not attack. Mafeking was facing a formidable army. The Boer forces, commanded by General Piet Cronje, "The Lion of the Transvaal," numbered about nine thousand men. They were equipped with the latest automatic rifles and machine guns, and were waiting for heavy artillery to be brought in from the Transvaal.

The Mafeking garrison of about 1250 men was not only outnumbered but badly equipped. Despite his pleas to military authorities in Capetown, Baden-Powell had not been able to get the weapons he considered necessary to defend Mafeking. There were enough automatic rifles for about half the town's troops; the rest of the men had been issued obsolete single-loaders. Mafeking had seven machine guns, and only four ancient, short-range cannons that could not fire as far as the main enemy laagers.

By the morning of October 16, the Boers had moved their heavy artillery into position. Just before 10 A.M. the telephone at B-P's command headquarters began to ring. Lookouts were calling in to report that the Boers were preparing to shell Mafeking.

The large gong outside command headquarters sounded loudly. It was answered by the railway iron on the verandah of Dixon's Hotel and by every church bell in town. Streets emptied as people raced for shelters, scrambled into trenches, vanished behind buildings and sandbags.

A distant BOOM . . . a high-pitched shriek . . . then a sharp explosion as the first shell landed on the outskirts of town. The bombardment continued for three hours.

But it was not as bad as everyone had feared. The enemy cannons were comparatively small and their range was poor. Many shells had fallen short of town. Those that landed inside Mafeking had exploded mainly in streets and backyards. Only two buildings had been hit, and the damage was slight. No one had been injured.

A short while later a Boer messenger walked across no-man's land, carrying a white truce flag and a message from General Cronje. He was escorted to B-P's headquarters. The message demanded the immediate surrender of Mafeking "to prevent further bloodshed."

B-P invited the messenger to lunch. Then he sent him back to his own lines with word that Mafeking's only casualty during the bombardment had been a chicken.

The Boers resumed their shelling the next morning, and from then on they bombarded the town for three or four hours every day. But they still hesitated to attack Mafeking directly.

Within a few days another Boer messenger came into town with an ultimatum from General Cronje. This time Cronje warned that he was waiting for a powerful, long-range cannon capable of destroying Mafeking. Unless the town surrendered within forty-eight hours, it would be leveled to the ground. B-P sent back a polite note thanking Cronje for the warning, rejecting his ultimatum, and warning him that Mafeking was surrounded by deadly landmines.

As Mafeking waited, alarming rumors spread through town. The new Boer cannon was so big, people said, it had to be drawn by sixteen oxen; the shells it fired were so heavy, it took four men to lift one of them. Shelters were reinforced, trenches dug a bit deeper.

On October 24, the Boers began to install their big siege gun at Jackal Tree, a heavily fortified enemy outpost about two miles south of town. Late that afternoon, Mafeking lookouts reported that the siege gun was being loaded. Alarms sounded, people ran for cover, and then the air vibrated with the impact of the loudest explosion Mafeking had heard so far. The first shell had fallen harmlessly into the veld. The next landed near the railway yards. Then shells began to explode all over town.

The Boers were firing a 94-pound siege gun—a big weapon, but not the giant everyone had feared. Thanks to Mafeking's excellent network of shelters and trenches, only two men were wounded by shrapnel and no one was killed. Since buildings in town were scattered over a wide area, property damage was surprisingly low.

Meanwhile, enemy patrols probing no-man's land had not encountered any of the landmines that were supposed to be buried there. At noon on October 25, after an intense morning bombardment, the Boers launched their first full-scale attack.

Troops manning Mafeking's outlying forts watched some two thousand enemy soldiers advance across the veld on horseback and by foot, coming from several directions and pulling small cannons along with them. B-P stood atop his lookout tower, field glasses glued to his eyes. A speaking-tube on the tower was connected to the telephone exchange down below; the exchange, in turn, was connected to each of the outlying forts. B-P instructed his men to stay under cover and hold their fire.

The Boers advanced closer, and still closer. Finally B-P grabbed his speaking-tube and gave the order: "Open fire!" A moment later, the British troops opened up with machine guns and rifles.

Hit by this sudden barrage, the advancing Boers hesitated in confusion as their officers shouted orders and waved the men on. The enemy troops plunged forward again, and the British kept on firing. Then the Boer lines wavered and broke. Abruptly, the enemy began to withdraw all along the front.

The entire action had lasted only a few minutes. One British soldier had been killed. Enemy losses were unknown, but were severe. Once again, Boer ambulance wagons rolled out onto the veld.

After this costly attack, the Boers changed their tactics. Now they began to dig trenches out into no-man's land, working at night and extending the trenches closer and closer to town.

On a moonless night near the end of October, B-P sent a squadron commanded by Captain "The Devil" Fitzclarence out across no-man's land. Fitzclarence's orders were to attack the Boer trenches with fixed bayonets, fire only if necessary, then withdraw as quickly as possible. To help the squadron find its way back in the darkness, red lanterns were hung on posts near the outskirts of town.

Bayonets drawn, Fitzclarence and his men reached the outermost Boer trench without being detected. A few minutes of noisy chaos followed . . . shouts, screams of pain, and finally rifle shots as the Boers tried to defend themselves in the darkness. When some of the Boers ran back toward their own lines, their comrades mistook them for British troops and opened fire on them. Meanwhile, the British squadron was already racing back toward the guiding string of red lanterns.

After that, B-P continued his game of bluff by hanging rows of red lanterns on the outskirts of town every few nights. The Boers, worried about another midnight bayonet charge, abandoned their efforts to approach Mafeking by digging trenches at night.

On October 31, the Boers attempted one more direct attack. This time they tried to capture Cannon Kopje, the crucial hill just south of town. Cannon Kopje was heavily manned and was defended with automatic rifles, two machine guns, and a small field cannon. About eight hundred enemy troops stormed the hill and approached to within six hundred yards of the British fort atop Cannon Kopje. Then, as wounded and dying Boer soldiers fell to the ground and tumbled down the hill, the enemy lines broke and the Boers retreated.

Defense of Cannon Kopje

By November 1, scores of Boer soldiers had died at the gates to Mafeking. Yet the enemy had failed to capture a single British outpost. The Boer commander realized that he could not force his way into Mafeking without losing too many men. There were other ways to subdue the stubborn little town, however. General Cronje decided to wait outside on the veld and bomb or starve Mafeking into submission.

Both sides settled down for a long siege.

Day after day Boer artillery shells whooshed across the veld, and in Mafeking the ground quivered with the impact of explosions. Spouts of earth flew into the air, sandbags bounced, windows shattered, walls crumbled and collapsed.

Sometimes shells landed in forts and trenches crowded with men.

There was no part of town, no part of the defenses, that Baden-Powell did not visit continually. He was up before dawn. With his aide-de-camp, he would ride out to inspect the outlying forts and talk with the men. During the day he was often seen standing atop his lookout tower, studying the enemy positions and watching for signs of a new Boer attack. Then he was gone . . . to confer with a staff officer, inspect the shelters, visit the hospital, listen to reports and complaints, or ride around the lines again.

The townspeople were reassured by the slight, wiry figure of the colonel, stationed on his watchtower or walking briskly through Market Square. He seemed so confident, and he had a cheerful word for everyone.

B-P did not often feel as cheerful as he appeared, however. African runners, sneaking through the Boer lines at night, brought news that British armies were being driven back all over South Africa. Relief forces might not reach Mafeking for months—if ever. Meanwhile, the town's food and ammunition supplies were dwindling. And Boer bullets and bombs were causing steadily mounting casualties.

As Commander-in-Chief, B-P knew that he must exhibit optimism at all times: he must try to keep up the spirits of the townspeople and garrison. Whatever personal doubts and anxieties he felt, he masked behind an encouraging smile and a jaunty manner.

He wanted every person in Mafeking to know exactly what was happening day by day. To begin with, notices were posted on bulletin boards throughout town. Before long, however, the four war correspondents who were stranded in Mafeking got together with the local printer and started the *Mafeking*

B-P's lookout tower

Mail, a newspaper which was "Issued Daily, shells permitting."

During the hours of shelling, the women and children were supposed to stay undercover. But it was impossible to keep some of the boys inside the shelters with their mothers and sisters. They were clamoring to take part in the town's defense.

Major Edward Cecil, B-P's Chief-of-Staff, suggested that a cadet corps of boys nine years or older be trained to take over some of the less dangerous but necessary jobs. These youngsters could then release additional men for the firing line.

To test his idea, Major Cecil organized a trial group of eighteen boys—a sergeant-major, a sergeant, two corporals, and fourteen privates. They were issued khaki jackets, which their mothers altered to size, and wide-brimmed hats like those worn by Baden-Powell and many of the men. They were trained to act as orderlies, carry messages, and take turns at lookout posts.

The idea worked, for the boys proved that they could make an important contribution to the defense of their town. Before long, every youngster old enough wanted to join the Mafeking Cadet Corps. Baden-Powell was impressed, and somewhat surprised, by the eagerness with which the cadets took on the responsibilities of men, and by their courage under fire.

One day a cadet delivered a message to B-P after riding his bicycle through heavy artillery fire. While the message was important, B-P was amazed at the boy's boldness. "You'll get hit one of these days," he warned, "riding about like that when shells are flying."

"I pedal so quick, sir," the boy replied, "they'll never catch me."

"These boys didn't seem to mind the bullets one bit," B-P wrote later. "They were always ready to carry out orders, though it meant risk to their lives every time."

Members of the Mafeking Cadet Corps

Shells rained on Mafeking from Monday to Saturday, but both sides had agreed to observe Sunday as a day of truce. At midnight Saturday all rifle and artillery fire stopped. For the next twenty-four hours, the people of Mafeking could walk freely through the shell-pitted streets of their town.

On weekdays, church bells tolling meant TAKE COVER! But on Sunday mornings the bells called the townspeople to church services. At noon, a band played in Market Square. Afternoons were usually devoted to outdoor events—races for the children, mule-driving contests for the men, football matches, cricket games, and gymnastic competitions. Sunday evenings were set aside for entertainments. The performers included everyone in town who could sing, dance, play a musical instrument, or tell a funny story, and many who couldn't. The people of Mafeking wanted to laugh. They wanted to forget the siege.

B-P never had a better chance to use his own talents as an entertainer. On Sunday evenings the Commander of the Mafeking garrison put on a circus director's uniform, called himself "Signor Paderewski," and acted as master-of-ceremonies. He sang popular songs from Gilbert and Sullivan operettas, and ridiculous songs he had written himself. And he performed comic skits that had made soldier audiences laugh years before in India, Afghanistan, Malta, and South Africa.

Across no-man's land, the Boers were also enjoying the Sunday truce. During the day they would leave their forts and trenches and stroll around the veld. B-P knew that the enemy forts were surrounded by barbed-wire; the wooden posts supporting the wire were visible through field glasses, and the Boer soldiers could be seen stepping carefully over the wire. The wire itself, however, could not be seen through field glasses.

Here was an opportunity for another bluff. There was no barbed-wire in Mafeking, but that didn't matter. If B-P couldn't see the Boers' wire, they wouldn't be able to see his. He had dozens of wooden posts made from poles, garden fences, and small trees. During the next week, these posts were put up in front of all the Mafeking defense forts.

"Then on Sundays," B-P wrote, "when our men stepped out to stretch their legs, they lifted them with the greatest care and difficulty over imaginary barbed-wire—a performance which greatly impressed the enemy watching them."

The barbed-wire ruse worked so well that Baden-Powell asked everyone in town to contribute other ideas for bluffing the enemy. One suggestion was to man the forts with life-sized dummies dressed as soldiers. These dummies were equipped with rifles fired by real soldiers, who then dropped into their trenches while the dummies drew the enemy's return fire.

Tricks like this helped confuse the Boers. Yet the fact remained that they were shelling Mafeking daily with long-range cannons, while the town's four small cannons could reach only half-way to the enemy lines.

One day one of B-P's staff officers, inspecting the western defenses, took a close look at a gate-post in front of a house near the outskirts of town. The gate-post, he discovered, was actually a cannon buried in the ground. When it was dug up, it turned out to be an ancient ship's cannon, which had apparently been brought to the area many years before.

The inscription on the cannon read: "B.P.—1770." This meant that it had been manufactured by the British gunsmiths Bailey, Pegg and Company in the year 1770. Everyone in town considered this a very good omen. They insisted that the initials really stood for "Baden-Powell," and that the cannon had belonged to him in a former life.

The newly discovered cannon was cleaned, oiled and mounted on a wooden carriage. Special cannon balls were made at the town's railway shops. Then the weapon was rolled down to the eastern front and tested. It proved to be in good working condition and was powerful enough to fire a ten-pound shell into the middle of a Boer laager. The puzzled Boers were forced to move their encampment farther back. Nicknamed "Lord Nelson," after the British naval hero, the cannon became an important part of Mafeking's defenses.

Major Panzera, the artillery officer who had made the "landmines" at the beginning of the siege, decided that if a 130-year-old cannon could be dug up and put into working condition, then it should be possible to build a brand-new cannon in the railway shops. Under Panzera's direction, the shop workers made a special furnace and used it to melt down some iron railings. When the railings were red-hot, they were twisted around a ten-foot-long locomotive steam pipe, until the pipe was completely surrounded by an iron casing. This was the barrel of the gun. In the railway foundry, workers cast a breech for the rear of the barrel and a metal trunion ring to support the barrel on a gun-carriage. Then they made sights and shells, mounted the gun on the chassis of a threshing machine, and rolled it to the front lines.

"It was a great day when we first fired the gun," B-P recalled. "She was loaded and set ready for firing, and then the gun's men and onlookers lay down under cover in case she should prefer to burst rather than send out the shell. But she didn't burst; she seemed to know what was wanted of her, and banged out the shell with a tremendous burst of smoke and flame! It was a grand success, and considerably astonished the Boers, who thought that we must have had a new gun sent up to us unknown to themselves."

Mafeking defenders and their homemade cannon "The Wolf"

The home-made cannon was nicknamed "The Wolf," after Baden-Powell's Matabele nickname, "The Wolf Who Never Sleeps."

General Cronje was getting impatient. After six weeks' siege, the stubborn town had not shown the least sign of surrender. "The garrison of Mafeking are not men," snapped Cronje. "They are devils."

Cronje decided that part of his force could be put to better use elsewhere. He withdrew from Mafeking with six thousand of his men, leaving the rest to wait out the siege.

The daily bombardments continued, and at Christmas Mafeking was still holding out. During the special Christmas day truce, food rationing was called off and simple gifts were distributed to the children. That evening the townspeople crowded into a large stable to enjoy what one of them called "a screamingly jolly entertainment."

New Year's Eve fell on a Sunday, and the usual truce was observed. Many townspeople attended midnight church services. No truce had been called for New Year's Day, however, so the troops remained at their posts. Baden-Powell spent the evening with his men, moving from one outpost to another in a steady, drizzling rain. At midnight, the Boers fired a few volleys into the air in honor of the year 1900. In Mafeking's outposts, soldiers raised their canteens to each other, drank toasts to the new century, and sang "God Save the Queen" and "Auld Lang Syne." Their voices rang out across the windswept veld as the Boer troops silently listened.

The shelling began again the next morning and lasted more than six hours, the heaviest barrage of the siege. Three people in Mafeking were killed on the first day of 1900.

Elsewhere in South Africa, British forces had met with several humiliating defeats. The Boers had advanced deep into British territory and had besieged two other towns: Kimberley in Cape Colony and Ladysmith in Natal.

By the end of January, however, reports were more encouraging. Reinforcements had arrived in South Africa from Great Britain and India, and British armies were finally beginning to drive back the Boers. In Mafeking, there was now hope that relief forces might reach the town before too long.

On February 8, a runner came into town with a message from Field-Marshal Lord F.S. Roberts, Commander-in-Chief of the British Army in South Africa. Roberts said that he could not relieve Mafeking until May.

The town had already endured four months of siege and its food, ammunition and medical supplies were dangerously low.

Baden-Powell put strict new rationing rules into effect. Every edible scrap of food had to be used. To avoid waste, communal dining halls were set up for everyone in town.

Until now there had been enough beef to go around. In February, horsemeat became part of the Mafeking diet. B-P had once read that Chicago meat-packing houses utilized every part of a slaughtered animal. "In Mafeking," he wrote, "we were not far behind Chicago, except perhaps in the matter of cleanliness. . . . Our by-products from slaughtered horses made a goodly list too: the manes and tails went to fill mattresses at the hospital, the hide after having the hair scalded off was boiled with the head and hooves to make brawn, the meat was cut off and minced, the interior arrangements were cut into lengths and used as sausage-skins for the mince, the bones and shreds of meat were boiled into soup, and the bones were then collected and pounded into dust and used for adulterating the flour, so the summing-up of the Chicago industry applies equally well to ours—namely, 'Everything pertaining to the animal was utilized except the squeal.' "

Oats, ordinarily used as horse-fodder, now became food for Mafeking's humans. Oat kernels were ground into flour for bread; the husks were used to make a thick, nourishing soup. The recipe for soup was: "Half a horse, 250 pounds; mealie meal, 15 pounds; oat husks, 47 pounds. This makes 132 gallons of soup the consistency of porridge."

As the siege continued, there was little animal life of any kind within Mafeking that did not find its way into the town's diet. When a swarm of locusts descended on the town, the people eagerly scooped them up and ate them fried, or boiled with curry.

The Boers, meanwhile, were again digging trenches across no-man's land, despite British efforts to stop them. By March, the trenches were so close to Mafeking's eastern defenses that enemy troops were able to spray the streets in that part of town with rifle fire.

British troops also began to dig trenches out into no-man's land. In some places they came within thirty yards of the enemy trenches. Both sides plunged into bloody trench warfare, exchanging shots at close range and charging with fixed bayonets. The Boers had an ample supply of hand grenades, but the British had none. Major Panzera, B-P's ingenious artillery officer, designed homemade grenades—meat and jam tins packed with gunpowder, with fuses attached. With the help of these grenades, the British finally forced the Boers to withdraw from their forward trenches.

Baden-Powell was now in constant touch with Colonel Plumer, commander of the Rhodesia regiment to the north. The town of Bulawayo, where Plumer had his headquarters, had not been attacked by the Boers, and since the beginning of the war, Plumer's regiment had been harassing enemy forces along the Rhodesia-Transvaal frontier.

In December, Plumer had moved south, intending to approach Mafeking and attack the Boers from the rear, but his regiment had been driven back. In March, he moved south again and this time reached a point only sixteen miles from Mafeking. On March 31 his men made a daring attempt to break through the Boer lines and reached the beleaguered town.

The attempt failed. The Boers learned of Plumer's advance, sent a large force to meet him, and managed to surround him. After losing many men, his regiment fought its way out of the Boer trap and returned to its base camp north of Mafeking. B-P heard that his old friend, Kenneth "The Boy" McLaren, who was Plumer's Chief-of-Staff, had been captured by the Boers. McLaren was badly wounded.

By April, British troops in South Africa were winning major victories. They had relieved the besieged towns of Kimberley and Ladysmith, had crossed the frontier into the Orange Free State, and were threatening the borders of the Transvaal.

On April 11, a runner came into Mafeking with a message for Baden-Powell from Queen Victoria. It was printed that day in the *Mafeking Mail:*

I continue watching with confidence and admiration the patient and resolute defense which is so gallantly maintained under your ever resourceful command.

Although Her Majesty was watching with confidence, Mafeking's supplies were almost gone. The siege was in its sixth month. Many soldiers and townspeople were suffering from dysentery, typhoid and diptheria. There wasn't enough nourishing food left to maintain the strength of fighting men already weakened by sickness.

B-P soon received another message from Field-Marshal Roberts, the British Commander-in-Chief. Relief forces moving north toward Mafeking were encountering fierce resistance; they might not be able to reach the town for another month.

At the end of April, the enemy troops surrounding Mafeking were reinforced, and during the first days of May, the shellings increased. Aware that British relief forces were drawing closer to the town, the Boers made one last desperate attempt to capture Mafeking.

At 4 A.M. on May 12, B-P was awakened by a stray bullet striking the wall of the verandah where he slept. He pulled on his uniform and rushed up to his lookout tower. Heavy artillery fire had broken out to the east of town. Rifle and machine-gun fire was coming from the west. The commander of the western defenses reported that three hundred enemy troops had forced their way into town and were advancing toward the African stadt.

B-P quickly sent a squadron of men to help close the western defense line and prevent more Boers from entering Mafeking. He dispatched another squadron to engage the enemy troops already inside the town. The invaders, unaware of what was happening behind them, continued to fight their way through the African stadt, setting fire to the thatched Baralong huts and advancing toward the British South Africa Police barracks.

From his watchtower, B-P saw enormous flames leap into the night, brilliantly illuminating the western part of town. He could hear shouts, screams and bursts of gunfire above the roaring and crackling of the flames. Hundreds of Baralong men, women and children were fleeing from the holocaust.

B-P tried to telephone the police barracks, but there was no reply. He tried again, then again. Finally a Dutch voice answered the phone. The Boers had captured the barracks and were holding Colonel Hore and seventeen of his men prisoner.

It was growing light now, and artillery fire to the east was increasing. Apparently, the Boers were preparing to launch a full-scale attack from that direction, but B-P realized that they were waiting for a signal from the enemy troops who had already entered Mafeking from the west. He now resorted to the most outrageous bluff of the entire siege.

He sent a messenger under a truce flag into the Boers' eastern lines with instructions to say that most of the enemy soldiers inside Mafeking had been killed or captured, while the others were surrounded. To avoid further casualties, the shelling should cease. Before long, hundreds of Boer troops emerged from trenches, hollows and ravines on the eastern front and returned to their laagers in the rear.

As this happened, B-P's troops were turning his bluff into reality. They had surrounded the police barracks, which was held by one party of Boers. The remaining Boer invaders had been split up into small groups; they were gradually killed, captured or driven back out of town. But the enemy troops who had captured the police barracks continued to hold out with their British prisoners.

Early that evening, B-P ordered his men to close in on the barracks. As they did, the door to Colonel Hore's headquarters flew open and the Colonel shouted, "Stop firing! Stop firing! The Boers have surrendered to me."

That same evening, a runner slipped into town with still another message from Field-Marshal Roberts. This time, it was the message Mafeking had waited seven months to receive. A British relief force of a thousand men, commanded by Colonel Mahon, was approaching Mafeking from the south. Colonel Plumer's Rhodesia regiment, with another thousand men, was still camped some sixteen miles north of town. The two forces would attempt to unite somewhere west of Mafeking and battle their way into town.

On May 16, heavy gunfire was heard to the west. The relief forces had apparently joined and had attacked the Boers.

"Some of us climbed up on to the high engine-sheds of the railway works for a better view," B-P wrote. "We could see the dust and smoke of the bursting shells in the distance, and even mounted men hurrying about from point to point. At last came the flick-flick of a heliograph [a mirror reflecting sunlight] through the haze—to which we promptly sent acknowledgment. Then we got the following:

"FROM X COLONEL X MAHON X HOW X ARE X YOU X GETTING X ON X.

"Then there was a pause of a long time. Again the flicker went on. WE X ARE X FIGHTING X HARD X BUT X GETTING X ON X WE X ARE X D X F X H X AND X —And that was the end of it—evidently the enemy interfered with their position. However, it was good enough for us. With a small party of men who had volunteered themselves as fit to march five miles (though we soon found that several could not do it) . . . we moved out to the front of Fort Ayer, and made a diversion against the rear of the Boers who were barring the advance of the Relief Force. This was late in the evening, and the Boers cleared away from being between two fires."

Soon afterwards, a messenger reached Fort Ayer with word that the relief force would enter Mafeking in the morning. B-P went back to his headquarters to get some sleep.

He didn't sleep long. At 3 A.M. he felt someone holding him by the shoulders and shaking him. He opened his eyes and saw his younger brother Baden grinning down at him. Major Baden Baden-Powell was Colonel Mahon's intelligence officer; he told B-P that Mahon and Plumer had changed their minds and had decided to enter Mafeking while it was still dark. Baden had come into town with an advance party so he could be the first to greet his brother.

B-P and Baden walked out to Fort Ayer. As they approached they saw "a whole crowd of men coming along in the darkness. It was the Relief at last!" There was no gunfire, for all the Boers on the western front had either surrendered or fled.

Later that morning, the two thousand man relief force left Fort Ayer and headed for town. Led by Colonels Baden-

Powell, Plumer and Mahon, they marched past the smoulder-
ing ruins of the African stadt, past houses with collapsed
chimneys, caved-in walls, and shattered windows. The town
Guard had mustered in Market Square to greet the relief column and cheer the Queen. "I have see many tributes to Her
Majesty," one of B-P's staff officers wrote, "but dirty men in
shirt sleeves and dirtier men in rags on scarecrows of horses
touched me most of all. We were dirty, we were ragged, but we
were most unmistakably loyal, and we came from all parts of
the world—Canadians, South Africans, Australians, Englishmen, Dutchmen, Arabians, Indians, and our Cape Boys and
various other Africans, and there was not one of us who did
not respect the other and know we were for the Queen and
Empire."

The cheering in Market Square lasted only a few minutes,
for there was mopping up to do. Enemy flags were still flying
over Boer laagers to the north and east of Mafeking.

The relief force began to shell the enemy encampments and
B-P rallied his own men for one final attack. By now, however, the Boers knew they were beaten. As British shells began
to fall, they hastily evacuated their laagers and took off for the
Transvaal frontier, eight miles away. When B-P and his men
reached the main Boer camp, it was deserted. Kettles of water
and pots of porridge were still boiling over breakfast campfires. Shouting and cheering exultantly, B-P's troops pulled
down the Boer flag and raised the Union Jack.

B-P rushed to the field hospital behind the Boer lines where
"The Boy" McLaren and thirty other wounded British soldiers had been held prisoner. All the wounded men were in
good enough shape to be taken to the town hospital.

Back in town, Market Square was now mobbed with people
who were "alternately cheering and choking down sobs." The

siege had lasted 217 days. B-P sent this message to Queen Victoria:

Happy to report Mafeking successfully relieved today. Northern and Southern columns joined hands on 15th. Attacked enemy yesterday, 16th, entirely defeating them with loss. Relieving forces marched into Mafeking this morning at nine. Relief and defense forces combined, attacked enemy laager, shelled them out, and took large amount of ammunition and stores. Townspeople and garrison of Mafeking heartily grateful for their release!

11

The Hero of Mafeking

THE TELEGRAM ANNOUNCING Mafeking's relief reached London shortly after 9 P.M. on May 18. At 9:20 the Lord Mayor posted a placard at the entrance to Mansion House, his official residence:

MAFEKING IS RELIEVED.
FOOD HAS ENTERED THE GARRISON.
ENEMY DISPERSED.

A large colored picture of Colonel Baden-Powell was hung over the balcony of Mansion House. Within minutes, the area in front of the Lord Mayor's residence was jammed with cheering men and women. His Lordship stepped out on the balcony and shouted:

"I wish the music of your cheers could reach Mafeking. For seven long weary months a handful of men has been besieged by a horde. (Cheers.) We never doubted what the end would be. (Tremendous cheering.) British pluck and valor when used in a right cause must triumph!"

Newsboys appeared on the streets shouting, "Extra! Extra! Mafeking relieved!" In sedate London restaurants, ladies and gentlemen waved their napkins, cheered Baden-Powell, and sang "For he's a jolly good fellow." In theatres and music halls, where evening performances were still underway, shows were interrupted and audiences sprang shouting to their feet as orchestras played "God Save the Queen" and "Rule Britannia." At the Hippodrome Theatre, Miss Lillian Lea sang a special ballad eulogizing the defense of Mafeking. The audience demanded eight encores.

Thus began what the London *Times* called "A remarkable demonstration of public enthusiasm. . . . No news in modern times has created more intense excitement. . . . The gallant defense of that little village on the open veld has moved the feelings of all the British people, and, indeed, of all the subjects of the Crown throughout the Empire. . . . The demonstration in London when the news was made known at the Mansion House was unparalleled in recent times. Nor was this surprising. There has been nothing like the defense of Mafeking in modern history."

Mafeking was a small frontier town. In terms of the larger war raging in South Africa, its strategic value was not great. It was neither as large nor as important as Kimberley or Ladysmith, which also had been besieged. But Mafeking had held out long after Kimberley and Ladysmith had been relieved. Its refusal to surrender had kept large numbers of Boers tied down when they might have been fighting elsewhere.

In the minds of both the British and the Boers, Mafeking had assumed a psychological importance far beyond its strategic value. Here, an out-numbered, poorly equipped, starving British garrison had defied the Boers in the face of overwhelming odds. Mafeking had become a symbol of British pride, courage and determination.

The streets of London were packed that night with a vast throng of roaring and flag-waving humanity. A *Times* reporter ventured out to join the crowds. When he finally got back to his desk he wrote:

"Colonel Baden-Powell must have heard the sound made by London last night. . . . At every step down Regent Street the excitement increased, and at Oxford Circus people were running in all directions and shouting. Down the broad thoroughfare I went with the stream, and on every omnibus people were waving flags and challenging the pedestrians with cheers and counter-cheers. The further I got down the street the thicker grew the throng and the wilder the excitement. Bands of young men and women flung past waving flags and shouting. . . .

"By this time the balconies and windows were alive with people, the pavement was almost impassable, and the vehicles had much ado to get along at all. At Picadilly Circus matters culminated. . . . The Circus was jammed with people. Then a cornet or some such instrument struck up "God Save the Queen." Immediately, thousands of voices took it up and in a twinkling every hat was off. It was a wonderful sight . . . the pavements and streets alive with cheering figures, and motionless among them the blocked streams of onmibuses and cabs

London celebrates the relief of Mafeking

all crowded with persons waving flags, hats, umbrellas, and anything they could lay their hands on. Every face wore a smile. No one minded being stopped or crushed. Ladies in evening dress were squeezed in the crowd, but only smiled happily. And over all and through it all the cheers thundered on in a continuous roar."

It was the same all over the British Isles. "From Brighton to the Pentland Firth, Britain went wild with joy." Britain also went wild with hero-worship. Pictures of Baden-Powell had appeared everywhere. On some buildings, red, white and blue lights spelled out the initials "B-P." Thousands of people gathered beneath the balcony of the Baden-Powell home near Hyde Park, singing and cheering until B-P's elderly mother appeared on the balcony, smiling and waving.

The newspapers could not praise Baden-Powell highly
enough. "No man in our day has done so much with such
slender means," said the *Times*. "None has shown a more
unquenchable cheerfulness in the presence of crushing dangers and cruel trials. None has displayed a greater fertility of
resource in devising expedients and turning to the best account the gradually dwindling powers of a half-starved popu-
lation. It is to the energy of Colonel Baden-Powell that we
owe the organization of a force which was able, not only to
hold Mafeking, but to keep the Boers back from raiding
Bechuanaland. . . . But, indeed, the gratitude and the admiration of the Empire must be given freely to all those—soldiers
and civilians, men and women, white and black—who bore
cheerfully and unflinchingly, during seven months, the priva-
tions and anxieties of the siege."

The people of Mafeking observed the end of the siege in
their own way. On May 18, a thanksgiving and memorial service was held in Market Square. The men of the relief force
stood at attention as Mafeking's threadbare garrison marched
past. Baden-Powell went around and thanked each unit for its
part in the town's defense. Mayor Whiteley delivered an emo-
tional speech. A clergyman paid tribute to those who had
given their lives. Some twenty thousand artillery shells had
fallen on Mafeking. Four hundred and eighty soldiers and
civilians had been killed by enemy bullets and bombs, or had
died of privation and disease.

As soon as the telegraph line to Capetown was reopened,
hundreds of messages reached the town. One of them, addressed to Baden-Powell, came from Queen Victoria:

I and my whole Empire greatly rejoice at the Relief of

Mafeking after the splendid defense made by you through all these months. I heartily congratulate you and all under you, military and civil, British and Native, for the heroism and devotion you have shown.

A few days later B-P received a telegram from the War Office, informing him that the queen had approved his promotion to the rank of major-general. At forty-three, he became the youngest general in the British Army.

Outside Mafeking, the war was still going on. British forces had captured Bloemfontein, capital of the Orange Free State, and were closing in on Pretoria, capital of the Transvaal. But the Boers, determined to keep on fighting, were breaking up into small guerilla bands. At the end of May, Mafeking returned to civil government and Baden-Powell was put in command of British forces in the northwest districts of the Transvaal.

That summer B-P's forces attempted to track down and capture Boer guerillas hiding in the Transvaal mountains. At the end of August, he was instructed to turn his command over to Colonel Plumer and report for a new assignment to Field-Marshal Roberts, the British Commander-in-Chief.

British officials believed that the war was approaching its end. Sir Alfred Milner, the British High Commissioner for South Africa, had suggested that a special police force be established to maintain order in the defeated Boer republics after a peace treaty was signed. Field-Marshal Roberts had recommended that Baden-Powell organize this force because of his "energy, organization, knowledge of the country, and a power of getting on with its people."

B-P reported to Roberts's headquarters, discussed the proposed police force with the Commander-in-Chief, then left for Capetown to confer with Sir Alfred Milner. As he traveled south on the train, crowds gathered at every station along the way to cheer the hero of Mafeking. He was rather surprised by all this commotion. The siege, after all, had ended more than three months earlier.

The day before his train reached Capetown he learned of "an unnerving ordeal which I should have to go through." The Mayor and other city officials were planning a mass cele-bration in B-P's honor. He tried to avoid this by telegraphing ahead that he would be a couple of days late. Even so, when his train pulled into the Capetown station, "The platform was a swaying mass of humanity, overflowing on to the roofs of neighboring trains, all cheering and waving.

"I have but a confused memory of what followed. I believe that a tiny space was cleared in which the Mayor was able to greet me with a short speech, and then I was bundled off, on the heads of a roaring mass, out of the station . . . and in this way I was—more or less upside down—carried through Cape-town all the way to Government House."

By October, B-P had drawn up plans for his police force, which would be called the South African Constabulary. He was to be Inspector-General of the force, and he faced a for-midable task. He had been given eight months to recruit, equip and train ten thousand men.

"We raked in men and officers wherever we could get them, all over the Empire," he wrote. "Stock-riders from Australia, farmers from New Zealand, cowboys from Canada, planters from India and Ceylon, constables from Ireland, and yeomen from England."

The purpose of the South African Constabulary was not simply to maintain law and order. Its mission was also to ease the transition from war to peace in the defeated Boer republics and help reconstruct those regions. B-P wanted a special kind of recruit. He wanted intelligent younger men who would respond to his own training methods, men who were likely to settle down in South Africa as useful citizens after their term of service ended. His requirements were so strict that only one out of every six applicants was accepted.

His training methods were similar to those that had proven so effective in India. The basic units of the Constabulary were troops of about a hundred men each; these troops were divided into six-man patrols, commanded by corporals who were largely responsible for training their men. Competitions among the patrols sharpened the men's efficiency and impressed each individual with the importance of his own contribution.

B-P designed the Constabulary uniform—a comfortable khaki shirt and breeches worn with knee-high boots; for more formal occasions, a khaki jacket was added. The uniform had facings of green and yellow—the colors of the Transvaal and the Orange Free State (and later the colors of the Boy Scouts). The hat was the wide-brimmed cowboy hat that B-P had found so useful in Ashanti and Matabeleland.

The men of the S.A.C. chose their own slogan: "Be prepared." This slogan expressed their readiness to take on any assignment; it also represented their commander's initials.

As B-P trained his Constabulary, guerilla warfare in South Africa lasted much longer than anyone had expected. Hundreds of Boer guerilla bands were still hiding in the mountains and carrying out surprise commando raids against British troops. Although the S.A.C. had been established to help maintain the peace, it was now called upon to take part in the guerilla war. As quickly as B-P's recruits were trained and equipped, they were sent into active duty.

By June, 1901, the S.A.C. had over nine thousand men fighting in South Africa. Raising this force in eight months was an impressive achievement, but it had been accomplished at the expense of Baden-Powell's health.

For the past two years he had been under constant pressure, and now he finally succumbed to exhaustion. An army medical board recommended that he be sent home on sick leave. He protested, but the doctors insisted. The S.A.C. would have to get along without him for a while.

He sailed from Capetown at the end of June. When his ship called at Madeira he was handed a telegram informing him that a reception was being planned for him at the English port of Southampton. He sent off a return telegram asking that the reception be canceled. When his ship reached Southampton, however, a cheering, flag-waving crowd was waiting to greet him.

A much bigger celebration was being planned in London, but B-P still was not accustomed to this sort of hero-worship. He arranged with railway officials to travel in a mail coach ahead of the regular passenger train to London and got off the mail coach just outside the city. Then he slipped off to visit his mother and sister in the town of Hindhead, where they were spending the summer.

He spent several weeks recuperating in England, visiting friends and relatives, and escaping attention by traveling under the name "Colonel Nicholson." When he regained his health, he began to accept invitations from some of the many cities and organizations that wanted to express their admiration for him. He realized now that as a national war hero, he could not refuse. One of the invitations he accepted came from Charterhouse. He visited his old school to dedicate a memorial in honor of Charterhouse alumni who had fallen in the war.

Another invitation came from King Edward VII, the son of Queen Victoria, who had died earlier that year. The King asked B-P to spend a weekend at Balmoral Castle in Scotland, so he could hear the General's own account of the siege of Mafeking. In recognition of B-P's war services, King Edward awarded him the Order of the Companion of the Bath.

When B-P left Balmoral Castle, the King presented him with a walking stick as a momento of his visit, and a haunch of venison as a reminder to keep up his health. "I have watched you at meals," the King said, "and I notice that you don't eat enough. When working as you are doing you must keep up your system. . . . Don't forget—eat more!"

By the time B-P returned to South Africa, the war was drawing to a close. The Transvaal and the Orange Free State had been devastated by months of bitter guerilla warfare, yet the Boers had continued to fight, determined to make the final British victory as costly as possible.

In May, 1902, Boer representatives finally asked to discuss peace terms. Their talks led to quick agreement, and the peace treaty was signed at the end of the month. The Transvaal and the Orange Free State became British crown colonies, with the promise of eventual self-government. Britain pledged three million pounds to help reconstruct the war-ravaged regions, yet the bitterness caused by this "unnecessary war," as many called it, would affect the political life of South Africa for generations to come.

The South African Constabulary was now able to undertake its original mission—keeping the peace and aiding in reconstruction. "I was really glad to have the job," B-P wrote, "since, long before the war, I had served in South Africa and had formed friendships with the South African Dutch. It was therefore distressing to find myself in the field against them. Now it was going to be my duty to help in pacifying the country and to be once more in friendly touch with them."

The officers and men of the S.A.C. took up permanent posts throughout the two new colonies, and as Boer families returned to their towns, villages and farms, the S.A.C. gradually won the confidence of these defeated people and helped them rebuild their lives. Besides maintaining law and order, members of the S.A.C. delivered mail, vaccinated babies, innoculated cattle, destroyed locusts, mediated local disputes, and made themselves generally useful. Most of the men learned the language of the country and were soon welcomed at every farmhouse.

By the end of 1902, B-P had covered some 13,000 miles by train and nearly 2500 miles on horseback inspecting the widely scattered S.A.C. stations.

Early in 1903 he was appointed Inspector-General of Cavalry—the highest cavalry rank in the British Army. This job would offer new challenges and another step forward in his army career. Yet he hated to leave the S.A.C., for he took great pride in his creation of this ten-thousand man organization, prepared to play a useful role in war or peace.

As Inspector-General of Cavalry, B-P lived up to his reputation as an officer with an independent mind and a willingness to try out new ideas. Soon after taking up his new post he began to visit cavalry training stations in other countries, seeking information and ideas that would help him improve the British Cavalry. He visited the United States for the first time to confer with American cavalry officers, tour Civil War battlefields, and inspect West Point. Later he made trips to France, Germany, Belgium, Austria, and Italy.

B-P as Inspector-General of Cavalry

Years before, he had watched army maneuvers in Austria and Italy as a spy. Now he attended cavalry maneuvers in these countries as an official guest.

He also traveled constantly through the British Isles on inspection tours. He had little use for traditional "spit-and-polish" inspections, when an army post spent weeks in feverish preparation and then put on formal drills, parades and displays for the inspecting general. B-P preferred to drop in on a cavalry regiment unexpectedly and simply ask the men to carry on with their regular activities. In this way he avoided all the window-dressing and was able to talk informally with the men, watch their training methods, and make suggestions for real improvements.

In 1906 he returned to South Africa for an inspection tour

of the cavalry regiments stationed there. At the end of his tour, he visited Mafeking for the first time since the siege.

His train pulled into town at 4 A.M., and since he had not told anyone when he would arrive, he was able to leave his baggage in the station and take a quiet walk through town. There were few signs of the siege left. Most of the damaged buildings had been repaired or replaced. The trenches and shelters were gone, the streets were paved now, and scores of new trees had been planted. Mafeking looked like a peaceful country town that had never known trouble. Yet B-P had not forgotten the bursts of machine-gun fire and the explosions of artillery shells. When a morning market cart rattled across some stones in the road, he instinctively ducked his head.

He spent several days in Mafeking, staying at the home of a former Town Guardsman and seeing many old friends and comrades. Then he returned to England by traveling northwards through Africa, visiting places he had never seen before.

Back in England he wrote an account of his African journey and combined it with his own first-hand description of the siege of Mafeking. This book, called *Sketches in Mafeking and East Africa,* was illustrated with dozens of B-P's water-colors and drawings.

His four-year term as Inspector-General of Cavalry expired in May, 1907. He was promoted to lieutenant-general and was placed in the reserves pending a new assignment. Meanwhile, his time was his own.

He already had a project in mind.

PART TWO

Peace Scout

12

Beginning a New Life

WHEN HE COMPLETED his term of duty as Inspector-General of Cavalry, Robert Baden-Powell could look back at thirty years filled with as much adventure and acclaim as any man could wish for. And he could look forward to the highest positions the British Army had to offer.

Many men would have been satisfied to continue such a career, enjoying its rewards and honors until they were ready to retire. But B-P was not such a man. At the age of fifty, with all the energy and enthusiasm of a boy, he was about to begin what he later called "my second life."

He did indeed live two distinct lives. And yet it is not really possible to point to a specific event or date and say, "Here is where his one life ended, and here is where the other began." Many things contributed to his new career as founder of the Boy Scout movement.

B-P's drawing of his "two lives"

B-P felt that an important turning point was his writing of the army manual called *Aids to Scouting*. It was published in England late in 1899, a few weeks after the Boers had besieged Mafeking.

Aids to Scouting was meant for soldiers, and thousands of copies were distributed to British troops. But it was no ordinary military manual, and it attracted the attention of people outside the Army as well. For one thing, it contained some fascinating stories about B-P's scouting adventures. For another, it presented a series of ingenious games and contests that could help an army scout develop his powers of observation, his ability to reason, and his memory. It showed a scout how to find his way across unfamiliar country, draw maps and sketches, follow tracks, keep himself hidden, and live off the land.

Many of the games and contests in *Aids to Scouting* could easily be practiced by anyone taking a walk through the country or a city park. The editors of a popular magazine called *Boys of the Empire* recognized the broad appeal of B-P's army manual, and in 1900 they reprinted parts of it for their young readers under the title, "The Boy Scouts." This was apparently the first use of the term "Boy Scout."

At the time, B-P was still in South Africa, organizing the South African Constabulary. When he came home after the war to take on his new post as Inspector-General of Cavalry, he was "astonished to find that my book was being issued in a great many schools." Schoolmasters were using *Aids to Scouting* to teach boys to observe, reason and remember—the same skills B-P had taught his army scouts.

He also found that some youngsters were forming their own scouting clubs. One boy wrote: "My two cousins and I have a B.P.S.S., that means Baden-Powell Scouting Society. We have had one try at it; it is hard to keep behind bushes without being seen, and we get horribly thirsty."

B-P had received thousands of letters from people all over the world since the siege of Mafeking. Many had come from boys and girls who wanted to express their admiration or ask his advice, and he had made it a point to answer each of them personally. Yet their letters made him wonder.

He had never really grown used to the idea of being a famous war hero. As Commander of the Mafeking garrison, he had simply performed his duty as best he could. Hundreds of other men had fought at Mafeking, and many had died there. In truth, every man, woman and child in that beleaguered little town had earned the right to be called a hero.

"My fame," B-P wrote, "gave me some anxious thought. It was all so unexpected, unearned, and unsought. Was it a call to me? Could it be utilized to some good end?

"These were the questions which thrust themselves upon me.

"They began to answer themselves for me by letters which poured in . . . from boys and girls in different parts of the

Empire. I had somehow personally caught their interest and was, without seeking it, in touch with them. . . .

"Here seemed an opportunity to do something, if only I knew what to do."

The opportunity came while B-P was still serving as Inspector-General of Cavalry, when he was invited to be Inspecting Officer at the annual Drill Inspection and Review of the Boys' Brigade. The Boys' Brigade was celebrating its twenty-first anniversary. It had been founded in Scotland by William Alexander Smith, an army lieutenant and a dedicated Sunday school teacher. Smith had been discouraged by the unruly behavior of many boys attending his Sunday school classes in a Glasgow slum, and since ordinary methods of discipline did not seem to work with these boys, he decided to try something new: he would combine religious education with military training. Perhaps he could drum some obedience into his students by putting uniforms on their backs and rifles in their hands.

The idea was surprisingly successful. Before long, boys who had been prowling the Glasgow streets in boisterous gangs were obediently drilling, marching, and parading.

As other Sunday school teachers followed Smith's example, the Boys' Brigade came into being and grew rapidly. By 1904, the organization claimed more than fifty thousand members in the British Isles. Its objectives were "the promotion of habits of Obedience, Reverence, Discipline, Self-Respect, and all that tends towards a true Christian manliness."

Seven thousand boys took part in the organization's annual Drill Inspection and Review, held at the Yorkhill Drill Ground in Glasgow on the afternoon of Saturday, April 30, 1904. Wearing smart uniforms and carrying wooden guns, the boys paraded across the field in perfect step, their heads erect, their backs straight, their arms swinging in unison. Then they performed a series of intricate drill maneuvers.

Baden-Powell, in his general's uniform, was mounted on a black charger as the boys marched past. Beside him, also on horseback, was Sir William Smith, the organization's founder. B-P turned to Smith and complimented him on the boys' fine performance. He hesitated a moment, then added: "Considering the number of boys in the country, you could have ten times as many members if the program you offered them was more varied and appealing."

"How would you make it more appealing?" Smith asked.

B-P told him how scouting had proved its popularity with young men in the Cavalry. He suggested that some form of scouting training might prove equally attractive to younger boys.

Smith nodded. "Perhaps you're right, General. Why don't you write a book for boys along the lines of *Aids to Scouting?*"

In the months following the Boys' Brigade Review, B-P thought a great deal about the training of boys. The parading boys in Glasgow had been alert, eager and well-disciplined, and B-P had been impressed. Even so, he was bothered by the uniforms and the toy guns, by the constant drilling and marching. The boys were playing at being soldiers.

B-P had spent his life training real soldiers, and he had little faith in formal military drill and rigid discipline. They might turn a man into an efficient robot, but they could not train him to think for himself or act on his own. If this was true of soldiers, it was certainly true of boys.

As an army officer, B-P had emphasized other types of training. Scouting and reconnaissance had proved particularly valuable because they encouraged each man to use his own initiative, to trust his own judgment. By giving a soldier definite responsibilities, scouting challenged him to do his best.

At Mafeking, B-P had learned that boys also responded eagerly to real responsibility, for the members of the Cadet Corps had played a valiant role in the defense of their town. "The conscientious way in which they did their work," B-P wrote, "opened my eyes to the fact that boys, if given responsibility and trusted to do their job, could be relied upon as if they were men. This was an important lesson for me."

His own boyhood provided another clue, for he still had vivid memories of the camping trips he had taken with his brothers. He remembered hiking across the fields and hills of England with a knapsack on his back, sailing through the Channel under a hot summer sun, watching for rabbits in the Copse at Charterhouse. Those wonderful days had helped prepare him for manhood.

He also remembered the butcher boys of Smithfield Market, who had carried on such a bitter feud with the young scholars of Charterhouse. The Smithfield boys had never had the opportunity to explore Britain's green hills, clear streams, and rocky shores. They had grown up amidst the rubble and soot of London's slums. What sort of men had they become?

Hundreds of thousands of boys were still growing up under much the same conditions. Some of them belonged to the Boys' Brigade and similar organizations, such as the Church Lads' Brigade. B-P felt that these organizations could do a great deal of good, yet the kind of training they used tended to encourage conformity, to force all boys into the same mould. Scouting, on the other hand, would stir a boy's imagination and appeal to his sense of adventure. It would challenge him to develop his own individuality.

If a boy practiced the skills of the pioneer, the explorer, the army scout, he would become more self-reliant and resourceful and would be prepared to make the most of his opportunities. If he learned to read the signs of the earth, understand the ways of animals, and fend for himself in the open, he would know the joy of being alive and aware in the world around him. If he ventured out to explore the wonders of nature, then he might discover wonderful things about himself.

These were some of the ideas B-P thought about as he traveled through the British Isles, inspecting cavalry regiments and attending army maneuvers. Two years passed before he found time to write out some definite suggestions and send them to Sir William Smith of the Boys' Brigade. He still had no thought of starting a separate scouting movement: he simply wanted to describe various ways in which scouting might be applied to the regular Boys' Brigade program.

His suggestions appeared in the *Boys' Brigade Gazette* in June, 1906, under the title "Scouting for Boys." This article presented a number of games and contests boys could practice in town or in the country. Some of these activities stressed observation, deduction and memory—basic skills of the army scout. In town, for example, a boy could "Look into five successive shop windows, one minute at each. Then write down the contents of, say, the 2nd and 4th from memory." Or he could "Look at six passers-by and describe from memory, say, the 2nd, 3rd and 5th, and what you reckon them and their business to be."

In city parks or in the country, a boy could learn to read tracks left by animals, people or carriages and try to guess the age and meaning of the tracks. Several boys could track each other; one of them could make tracks with footprints or a walking stick, or he could leave behind signs such as bits of paper or cloth. B-P asked his readers to "use your power of noticing details to spot people in everyday life who need help, and to help them in however small a way."

Other suggested activities dealt with such practical outdoor skills as distance-judging, finding the way with a compass or by the stars, lighting a fire with only two matches, cooking without utensils, first-aid, and life-saving. Instead of the formal calisthenics favored by the Boys' Brigade, B-P suggested hiking, racing and swimming. All the games and contests he described were designed for individual boys or small groups, in place of the large companies which practiced drill and marching in the Boys' Brigade.

He was still working out his ideas. The next step was to take up Sir William Smith's challenge and write a scouting handbook especially for boys.

To begin with, B-P wanted to know how boys in other cultures and at other times in history had prepared for manhood. He read about the training of youth in ancient Greece and Japan, the education of young pages, squires and knights in medieval Europe, the instruction given young Zulus in Africa, Polynesians in the South Seas, Indians in North America.

He also studied all the important boys' organizations in England—including the Boys' Brigade, the Church Lads' Brigade, Lord Rodney's Cadets, and Forbush's Knights of King Arthur. Finally, he investigated two popular boys' movements in the United States—the Woodcraft Indians founded by Ernest Thompson Seton, and the Sons of Daniel Boone founded by Dan Beard. Both these movements stressed nature study and outdoor skills and came very close to B-P's own ideas about the effective training of boys.

Early in 1907 he wrote two four-page leaflets called *Boy Scouts, A Suggestion* and *Boy Scouts, Summary of a Scheme.* These leaflets pointed out that scouting was "a novel and attractive form of training." It would appeal to "boys of all creeds and classes." And it could be applied to "any existing organization for boys, such as Schools, Boys' Brigades, Cricket Clubs, Cadet Corps, etc., or it can supply an organization of its own where these do not exist."

B-P sent copies of the leaflets to a number of friends, educators, and youth leaders. About this time he met Cyril Arthur Pearson, owner of several large daily newspapers and a popular weekly magazine. Pearson had expressed interest in the Boy Scout scheme and wanted to publish B-P's new handbook, which would be called *Scouting for Boys.* He was in a position to distribute the handbook throughout the British Isles at a price low enough to enable any boy to buy a copy.

B-P and Pearson made arrangements to publish the book and also agreed to start a new weekly magazine called *The Scout.* Since the handbook and the magazine would probably result in many requests for information about scouting, the publisher offered to supply a small office in London and a full-time secretary. B-P asked his old friend Kenneth McLaren, who had recently retired from the Army, to take over the management of this office.

After his term as Inspector-General of Cavalry was over, B-P worked full-time on the first draft of *Scouting for Boys,* while awaiting his next army assignment. Before completing the book, however, he wanted to see how a group of boys would react to a real scouting expedition.

He selected twenty-one boys—the world's first Boy Scouts. On an island off the coast of Britain they were to spend a week at the world's first Boy Scout camp.

13

Brownsea Island

BROWNSEA ISLAND GUARDS the entrance to Poole Harbor, on the southern coast of England. Roman galleys landed here two thousand years ago when Britain was a remote outpost of the Roman Empire. Later, King Canute of the Danes used the little island as a base to attack and conquer the mainland beyond. Then the island became a refuge for some of the most notorious pirates and smugglers along the Channel coast.

King Henry VIII put an end to the smuggling. In 1520 he had a fortress built on the island's eastern tip, so his royal guards could watch all ships entering and leaving Poole Harbor. Brownsea Island remained Crown property for the next two centuries and was finally sold to private owners.

Baden-Powell knew the island, for he had visited it as a boy on sailing trips with his brothers. They would land secretly on one of its sandy beaches, go swimming, and explore its open fields and pine-clad hills.

When B-P began to plan his first Boy Scout camp, the island was owned by Mr. and Mrs. Charles van Raalte, a wealthy couple who had built a summer home there. B-P met the van Raaltes early in 1907, told them about his scouting idea, and suggested that Brownsea Island would be an ideal spot for his experimental camp. The van Raaltes agreed. They invited B-P to bring a group of boys to their island during the coming August holidays.

Once he had found a suitable camping spot, B-P began to choose his campers. He was anxious to see how scouting would appeal to boys of different backgrounds, and how those boys would get along with each other.

He invited the sons of several well-to-do friends, boys who attended Eton, Harrow, and other exclusive boarding schools. Then he asked the Boys' Brigade companies in Poole and Bournemouth, just across the harbor from Brownsea Island, to select some of their members for the camp; these boys were the sons of local shopkeepers, craftsmen, farmers and fishermen. A third group of campers came from the slums of London's East End, and by inviting these boys, B-P remembered the Smith-field butcher lads of his own boyhood.

Altogether he invited twenty-one campers between the ages of eleven and sixteen. His nine-year-old nephew, Donald, pleaded to go along too. B-P felt that Donald was too young to take part in the camp's activities, but he agreed to let the boy attend as an "orderly." Then he asked his friend Kenneth McLaren to help him run the camp.

Boys' Brigade officials in Poole and Bournemouth got to-gether the necessary equipment—such things as tents, bed-ding, cooking gear, tools, and boats. The boys would do some cooking themselves, but to assure wholesome meals—and to reassure their worried parents—B-P hired a professional cook to ship food out to the island every day.

On July 29, 1907, B-P, his nephew Donald, and the boys from the London area took a train to Poole, crossed to the island by motor launch, and landed at Brownsea pier. Then they hiked a half-mile along the shore to the campsite B-P had picked out. McLaren was already there with the boys from Poole and Bournemouth.

The campsite, a level area overgrown with blue heather and

yellow gorse, looked out across the harbor toward the mainland. Behind it rose a wooded hillside. An abandoned brick building once used to make pottery stood at one end of the site and would provide a useful storehouse. Nearby were two shallow ponds and a fine sandy beach.

B-P, McLaren, and the boys set to work clearing the ground and pitching tents. In the center of the campsite, the boys put up a tall flagpole and raised the Union Jack. B-P pushed one of his old pigsticking lances into the ground outside his own tent and attached the tattered flag that had flown over his Mafeking headquarters.

He had found that the best way to train army scouts was to divide them into small, independent units. He followed this same system with his campers, organizing them into four "patrols"—*Wolves, Bulls, Ravens,* and *Curlews*—which would compete against each other in games and contests. The oldest boy in each patrol was named "patrol leader." And the four patrols together formed a "troop."

"Each patrol leader was given full responsibility for the

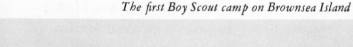

The first Boy Scout camp on Brownsea Island

behavior of his patrol at all times, in camp and in the field,"
B-P wrote later. "The patrol was the unit for work and play, and
each patrol was camped in a separate spot. The boys were put
'on their honor' to carry out orders."

Although the boys had brought ordinary street clothing
with them, B-P devised a makeshift uniform. Each camper
pinned a long streamer of brightly colored wool to his left
shoulder—blue for *Wolves,* green for *Bulls,* red for *Ravens,*
and yellow for *Curlews.* And each patrol leader was issued
a small flag with a picture of the patrol animal painted on it.

All the boys received long wooden staffs of the kind B-P had
found so useful for jumping streams, testing the ground, and
taking measurements during the Ashanti campaign. And each
boy was given a fleur-de-lys badge to pin to the front of his
cap—the same badge that B-P had awarded successful gradu-
ates of his army scouting course in India. Slightly altered, it
would soon be known the world over as the Boy Scout Badge.

By the evening of July 31, everything was ready. After dinner the boys gathered around their first campfire. B-P explained the program for the week ahead and then told about
some of his own scouting adventures. A half-century later, in
1957, one of the campers still remembered that first campfire
on Brownsea Island.

"B-P was a wonderful teller of tales," wrote Sir Humphrey
Noble, who had been a member of the *Ravens* Patrol, "and he
had had the most exciting adventures and escapes during his
army life. He had a very clear resonant voice which arrested
attention from the very first. So you can imagine us sitting
there in the darkness around the fire, listening spellbound to
some thrilling story."

At six the next morning, B-P blew reveille on a giant

koodoo horn he had once found in South Africa. The campers tumbled out of their tents, washed up, and raced for the big army tent that served as a dining room and meeting place in rainy weather. After breakfast, the day's activities began.

Tracking was the first activity. At the campfire the night before, B-P had described some of his own tracking experiences and had explained that tracking requires close observation and clever reasoning. Now, he and McLaren taught the boys how to recognize and interpret various kinds of tracks. Were they made by a person, an animal, or a vehicle? By one person or several? How big was the person? Was he walking or running? How old were the tracks? Where did they lead? What did they mean?

That morning the boys practiced making tracks and reading them. Afterwards, they took part in a variety of tracking games and contests.

One game was called "Deer Stalking." Each patrol picked one of its members to be the "deer." He was given a half-dozen tennis balls and was sent off into the woods. Twenty minutes later the rest of the patrol, the "hunters," took off after him and attempted to follow his tracks. Each hunter was armed with one tennis ball. The deer hid in the woods and tried to ambush the hunters. If he hit a hunter with a tennis ball, the hunter was "gored" and was out of the game. If the deer was hit by three balls, he was "killed."

The boys—creeping through the woods, watching for tracks, hiding behind trees, shouting and chasing, throwing and ducking—were having a marvelous time. Deer Stalking was an exciting game, but it was also part of a program that B-P had worked out very carefully in advance to teach his campers the skills of the frontiersman, the explorer, the army scout.

That week the campers stalked animals, blazed trails,

B-P and some Brownsea Island campers

judged distances, and found their way with a compass and by the stars. They made fires, built huts in the woods, laid bridges across streams, and sent signals with smoke, flags, and reflected sunlight. They learned to tie knots and recognize plants and trees, they had running, jumping, swimming, boating, tug-of-war, and ju-jitsu contests, and they played Lion Hunting, Spot the Thief, Dispatch Running, Siberian Manhunt, and Old Spotty Face. One day the chief officer of the local coastguard came to the island to instruct the boys in lifesaving, first-aid, and fire-fighting.

Every evening one of the patrols went on night bivouac. Carrying blankets, rations, and cooking gear, the boys hiked to some lonely spot, built a fire, and cooked their supper. Then they would post sentries. Later that evening, B-P and some of the other campers, acting as "enemy scouts," would seek out the bivouac and try to sneak past the sentries.

B-P had taught the boys always "to look up" when scouting, as well as watching on all sides. One night, however, as he crept through the woods, he forgot to observe his own rule.

Suddenly he heard the loud crashing of branches above his head. A small figure leaped out of a tree and shouted, "Halt! Hands up!"

It was Donald Baden-Powell, who had refused to be simply an "orderly," and who now had the distinction of capturing his own uncle. B-P raised his hands, and with Donald behind him, marched obediently off to the night bivouac.

The best part of the camp for most of the boys was the evening campfire, when they gathered around that circle of warmth and friendship glowing in the darkness. Percy W. Everett, the editorial manager for B-P's publisher, visited Brownsea Island and later described one of the campfires:

"I can see [B-P] still as he stands in the flickering light of the fire—an alert figure, full of the joy of life, now grave, now gay, answering all manner of questions, imitating the call of birds, showing how to stalk a wild animal, flashing out a little story, dancing and singing around the fire, pointing a moral, not in actual words but in such an elusive and yet convincing way that everyone present, man or boy, was ready to follow him wherever he might lead."

One night B-P told the campers about that hot, steamy day in South Africa, twenty years before, when he had met the impressive army of Zulu warriors led by the bearded Scottish trader, John Dunn. He still remembered the wonderful anthem sung by those warriors as they marched over the crest of the hill. Now he taught his campers the same song, and a Zulu war dance to go along with it.

"Een-gonyama Gonyama!" B-P sang.

"He is a lion—a lion!"

And his campers shouted back: *"Invooboo! Yah-bo! Yah-bo! Invooboo!"*

"Yes! He is better than that! He is a hippopotamus!"

The boys lined up around the campfire; each boy held his wooden staff in his right hand and placed his left hand on the shoulder of the boy in front. Then they moved forward a few steps, singing the *Invooboo* chorus and stamping their feet in unison. They repeated the chorus, and this time they moved a few steps backward. The third time they formed a wide circle, still stamping their feet and shouting, *"Invooboo! Yah-bo! Yah-bo! Invooboo!"*

One of the boys jumped into the center of the circle and performed a dance, showing how he had stalked and killed a wild buffalo. As he crept up on the beast, the boys surrounding him crouched low and whispered the *Invooboo* chorus. The hunter approached his prey and then sprang. The other boys leapt up, shouting and stamping wildly.

Now, each boy in turn entered the circle to stalk a wild beast. The campfire roared and crackled and sent up sparks, throwing weird shadows on their dance, and the boys' voices rang out through the night.

And when the last boy had triumphed, everyone cheered and shouted until they fell laughing in a tangled heap. The laughter died away as B-P stood before them again, grinning at first, but then grave as he began his closing story. Once more the campers sat around the fire, leaning forward a bit, their arms wrapped around their knees, listening silently to their famous leader as nightjars burred in the pine trees behind them, and waves slapped gently on the beach below.

The last full day of camp, the boys had a chance to demonstrate what they had learned. B-P had invited the parents of the local campers and other interested adults to watch a show planned by the campers themselves. Afterwards, Mr. and Mrs. van Raalte asked everyone to their summer home on the island. As the crowd ate supper in the van Raaltes' dining room, a brass band from Poole played on the terrace.

The last campfire was held that evening. The next morning the boys helped strike camp.

The world's first Boy Scout camp was over. The first Boy Scouts climbed reluctantly into motor launches and sailed back across the harbor, returning to Poole and Bournemouth, to Eton and Harrow, and to the slums of London's East End.

It had been an unforgettable week for the campers—pioneers in an adventure that millions of other boys soon would share.

14

Scouting for Boys

"I AM GOING to show you how you can learn scoutcraft for yourself and put it into practice at home."

This promise appeared in the opening pages of *Scouting for Boys,* the handbook that was to introduce Baden-Powell's scouting program first in Great Britain and later in the rest of the world. B-P and his publisher had decided to issue the handbook in six paperback installments, which would appear on bookstalls and newstands every other week. Afterwards, the complete book would be published in an inexpensive clothbound edition.

Part I appeared on January 15, 1908. It resembled a pocketsize magazine, sold for four pence (ten cents) a copy, and was described on the title page as "A Handbook for Instruction in Good Citizenship."

The booklet began with a Foreword for Instructors. "By the term 'Instructor,'" wrote B-P, "I mean any man or lad who takes up the training of either a Patrol (six to eight boys), or a Troop (several patrols joined together). By means of this book I hope that everyone, even without previous knowledge of scouting, may be able to teach it to boys—in town as well as in the country."

Instead of presenting his scouting program in ordinary text-book fashion, B-P had written a series of entertaining Camp Fire Yarns, similar to stories he might have told around the campfire at Brownsea Island. The first yarn opened with a description of the "Mafeking Boy Scouts" who had come so eagerly to the defense of their town. B-P then told about the work of various kinds of "peace scouts"—frontiersmen, explorers, pioneers, missionaries, and so forth. Peace scouting, he said, was both an exciting outdoor adventure and a challenging way to become a useful member of one's own community. "You need not wait for war in order to be helpful as a scout," B-P wrote. "As a peace scout there is lots for you to do, wherever you may be."

This Yarn ended with "A good example of what a Boy Scout can do." The example was a condensation of *Kim,* Rudyard Kipling's story about a boy whose intimate knowledge of India makes him a valuable asset of the English Secret Service.

The second Camp Fire Yarn introduced B-P's Boy Scout program: "To become a Boy Scout you join a patrol belonging to your Cadet Corps, or Boys' Brigade, or club. If you are not a member of one of these, or if it does not as yet possess a patrol of scouts, you can raise a patrol yourself by getting five

Part I.   Price 4d. net

SCOUTING
FOR BOYS ^{BY} B-P

LIEUT. GEN.
BADEN POWELL C.B.

PUBLISHED BY HORACE COX,
WINDSOR HOUSE, BREAM'S BUILDINGS, LONDON E.C.

Cover design by John Hassall

Part I of Scouting for Boys

other boys to join. They should, if possible, be all about the
same age. One boy is then chosen as Patrol Leader to command the patrol, and he selects another boy to be the corporal
or second in command. Several patrols together can form a
'Troop' under an officer called the 'Scoutmaster.' "

B-P went on to describe the sort of things a Boy Scout
learned—nature lore, observation and deduction, tracking,
stalking, camping in the open, laying fires, tying knots, signaling, pathfinding, and so on. Along with these outdoor skills, a
Scout was also expected to know about good health practices,
physical fitness, first-aid, life-saving, patriotism, and what B-P
called "Chivalry," or helping others. "One of the chief duties
of a Scout," he wrote, "is to help those in distress in any
possible way you can." This Yarn ended with "The Elsdon

Mystery," a story about an observant boy detective who uses scouting skills to solve a murder mystery.

The Third Camp Fire Yarn dealt with practical matters important to any future Scout. It set forth the tests and qualifications for second- and first-class Scout, for three badges of honor (in signaling, stalking, and first-aid), and for special life-saving and meritorious-service medals. It presented the Scout Oath and Scout Motto, and it described the Scout salute, Scout songs, secret calls and signs, and the Scout Badge, described by B-P as "the arrow head, which shows north on the compass."

The fourth Camp Fire Yarn presented the Scout Law.

These four Yarns were followed by instructions for several scouting games and contests. The booklet ended with a "Scout's play," accompanied by directions for making the costumes and scenery.

The next five installments of *Scouting for Boys* were similar to Part I but dealt in much greater detail with the scouting activities B-P had already outlined. All six installments were published as a complete book on May 1, 1908. By the end of the year, this book had been reprinted five times and was already being translated into several languages.

It was translated into dozens of languages as scouting spread overseas, and was also expanded and revised many times to keep pace with a growing Scout movement and a changing world.

In the United States, *Scouting for Boys* was eventually replaced by another handbook written to meet the particular needs of the Boy Scouts of America. In several other countries, Scout associations also developed their own special handbooks. And in Great Britain, a new, up-to-date handbook was recently issued for British Scouts.

Yet all these modern handbooks stem directly from the original version of *Scouting for Boys,* which emphasized outdoor life and service to others and thus presented the essentials of scouting as it is still practiced today.

The first issue of *The Scout* magazine, meanwhile, had appeared on April 18, 1908. Priced at a penny a copy, it featured mystery and adventure stories by popular boys' writers of the time, along with articles on such subjects as "Why Scouts Must Keep Fit," "Things All Scouts Should Know," "How to Become a Scout," and "The Best Dog for Scouting." But the highlight of this first issue was an article written by B-P, called "How Scouting Started."

"I have suggested scouting as a good thing for boys because I began it myself when I was a boy," he wrote. B-P told about the hiking and boating trips he had taken with his brothers, and about his experiences in the Copse at Charterhouse. Then he described some of his adventures as an army scout. Finally he explained how the idea of peace-scouting had occurred to him:

"Some years ago I wrote a little book of scouting instruction for soldiers in the cavalry, and when I came home after the war I was astonished to find that this book was being issued in a great many schools. So I thought how much better it would be if I wrote a book about peace-scouting for boys. . . .

"By forming 'patrols' of scouts in different places I hope to get all the different boys' clubs to come into close touch with each other, and for all boys to be scouts, and therefore useful men and good friends among themselves."

By the time all six installments of *Scouting for Boys* had appeared, B-P had been recalled to active military duty. Great Britain was organizing a new Territorial Army made up of volunteers who would be trained to support the Regular Army in wartime. Lieutenant-General Baden-Powell had been put in command of the Northumbrian Division of the Territorials.

For the next two years he led a hectic double life. He spent much of his time in the north of England, transforming the raw recruits of his Northumbrain Division into an effective fighting force. Meanwhile, he kept in constant touch with Scout headquarters in London and wrote a regular weekly column for *The Scout* magazine. Whenever possible, he met with youth leaders who had expressed an interest in his program, and he visited some of the thousands of Scout patrols and troops that were being formed all over the British Isles.

Neither B-P nor anyone else could have foreseen the enthusiasm with which boys took up scouting. The idea caught on so quickly that at first it was difficult to keep track of the movement's growth. By the end of 1908, some sixty thousand boys had registered as Scouts and were invading Britain's parks and countryside, broomstick staffs in one hand, dog-eared copies of B-P's handbook in the other. By the summer of 1909, there were more than 100,000 registered Boy Scouts in Great Britain and the little headquarters office in London was being overwhelmed with letters asking advice and assistance.

What was it that made this new idea so appealing to so many boys? For one thing, Baden-Powell's name alone was enough to catch the attention of boys all over Britain, for he was still greatly admired as a national hero. But if many youngsters read *Scouting for Boys* just because of B-P's reputation, it was his scouting program that captured their enthusiastic participation.

At the time, there was no such thing as a widespread camping movement for boys. Those few boys who camped in the open, as B-P and his brothers had done, did so on their own. Now B-P was offering all boys an opportunity to lead the self-sufficient lives of explorers, frontiersmen and pioneers. Follow me, he said, and we'll pitch our tents under the open sky. We'll light fires, cook our own grub, send signals, and read the meaning of tracks and signs. We'll find our way by the sun and stars and blaze trails through the wilderness.

Scouting answered a boy's craving for fun and adventure. But its appeal ran deeper than that, for it also spoke directly to a boy's self-respect. Instead of imposing a lot of rules, scouting put a boy on his honor and trusted him to do his best. It encouraged him to follow his own special interests and discover his own unique abilities. It asked him to use his skills and knowledge to help others. And it challenged him to take on a man's responsibilities.

Scouting took boys seriously, and that was the real secret of its enormous appeal.

The first issue of *The Scout* magazine had announced a contest to select thirty boys for "The Most Fascinating Holiday Ever Offered"—two weeks at a summer camp with Baden-Powell. The camp was held in August, 1908, at Humshaugh, Northumberland, not far from B-P's Territorial Army headquarters. It differed from the one at Brownsea Island because the campers, called the "Gallant Thirty," were all members of patrols at home and were familar with the scouting program.

Since the ordinary street clothing worn at Brownsea Island hadn't been very practical, B-P had now designed a comfortable, inexpensive uniform that would be suitable for all scouting activities. This first Boy Scout uniform was based on the one B-P had found so serviceable as an army scout. It included

Drawing of B-P's first Boy Scout uniform

a wide-brimmed cowboy hat, khaki shirt and shorts, a brightly colored neckerchief, and long black stockings. The wooden staff B-P had first used in Ashanti also became an essential part of that early uniform.

The Scout magazine held another contest in 1909, and an important new activity entered scouting. This time one hundred boys attended a summer camp under B-P's leadership on the southern coast of England. Since a scouting enthusiast had offered the campers the use of his yacht, the *Mercury,* the camp was held partly on land and partly at sea. During the first week, half the boys lived aboard the *Mercury* while the others camped on land. The next week the two groups changed places. From then on, Sea Scouting was part of the regular scouting program. B-P asked his eldest brother Warington, who was still an expert yachtsman, to write the official handbook, *Sea Scouting.*

That same summer, the first large scouting event was held at the Crystal Palace Exhibition Hall in London to give the British public a chance to see scouting in action. Ten thousand boys took part, demonstrating scouting skills and activities by means of exhibits and competitions.

While B-P was touring the Crystal Palace Rally, he came upon a group of seven girls wearing white blouses, blue skirts, and long black stockings. They also had wide-brimmed hats and bright scarves, and they carried long Scout staffs.

"Who are you girls?" B-P asked.

A perky eleven-year-old stepped forward and announced, "We are the Girl Scouts."

Several thousand girls had already registered as Boy Scouts at London headquarters, but there was no clear-cut place for them within the Scout movement. B-P felt that they deserved an organization of their own. Soon afterwards he discussed this idea with his mother and sister; then he asked Agnes to help him start a new movement for girls. He suggested calling this movement the Girl Guides—since a guide, like a scout, knows the right path and can lead others. (In the United States, the girls' movement, founded by Mrs. Juliette Low, has always been known as the Girl Scouts.)

A few weeks after the Crystal Palace Rally, King Edward VII invited B-P to spend another weekend at Balmoral Castle in Scotland. When B-P arrived at the castle, Colonel Legge, the King's equerry, escorted him to the royal chamber. As they approached the door, the Colonel paused for a moment and attached two safety pins to B-P's jacket. He instructed one footman to bring a cushion, and another to bring a sword.

"It was like preparation for an execution," B-P wrote.

"Then we walked in. The King, in Highland dress, shook hands, smiling most genially, and kept hold of my hand while he told me that for my many services in the past and especially for my present one of organizing the Boy Scouts for the country, he proposed to make me a Knight Commander of the Victorian Order.

"He then sat down and I knelt on the cushion in front of

him, the equerry handed him the sword and he tapped me on each shoulder and hung the cross round my neck and hooked the star of the Order on my coat, and gave me his hand to kiss. Then he laughingly told me that his valet would put the ribbon right for me, and out I went."

With this ceremony, B-P became a knight. From then on his title was Sir Robert Baden-Powell.

B-P had never meant to start a new organization. He had intended that scouting "be used as an additional attraction by those in charge of boys' organizations of any kind. If it is taken up by several, it may prove a bond between all."

Yet scouting had its own special appeal, and despite B-P's intentions, it was rapidly becoming an independent movement. Tens of thousands of boys who did not belong to established organizations were forming their own patrols and troops, often without any supervision or control. They wanted to be Boy Scouts, and nothing else.

With these boys in mind, B-P wrote to a number of prominent men who had expressed an interest in scouting and asked them to set up local volunteer committees throughout the British Isles. These local committees would register all Scout patrols and troops in their districts. They would also set qualifications for Scoutmasters, regulate the awarding of Scout badges and medals, supervise local camps and rallies, and help form new patrols and troops.

Meanwhile, several established boys' organizations in Great Britain were experimenting with scouting, but not too successfully. The difficulty was that the Boys' Brigade, the Church Lads' Brigade, and other large groups had their own ideas about training boys, and their ideas did not always fit in with the expanding Scout program.

Most boys' organizations in Britain at the time were affiliated with certain churches. They stressed religious instruction as part of their programs. B-P insisted that scouting be open to boys of all religious beliefs—not just certain ones. "We are *inter-denominational,*" he wrote. "We do not assume or interfere with the prerogative of parents or pastors by giving religious *instruction,* but we do insist on the observance and practice of whatever form of religion the boy professes."

B-P added that scouting also welcomed boys who did not practice any religion. He felt that the scouting program, with its code of honor and its ideals of service, could be especially helpful to these boys.

Along with religious instruction, the Boys' Brigade and the Church Lads' Brigade emphasized military training and mass drill. B-P had been disturbed by this from the beginning, and as his movement grew, he became even more convinced that scouting had no place for military training. Scouting had been founded by a soldier, yet its whole intention was to train boys for peaceful citizenship.

"Our training," he wrote, "is non-military. Military drill tends to destroy individuality, whereas we want, in the Scouts, to develop individual character; and when once drill has been learned it bores a boy who is longing to be tearing about on some enterprise or other. . . . Our aim is to make young backwoodsmen of [the boys], not imitation soldiers."

It soon became clear that a separate organization was needed to guide the development of the Boy Scout movement. The first step toward such a organization had been the formation of the local volunteer committees throughout Great Britain. The next step came at the end of 1909, with the establishment of a national committee of volunteers, called the Governing Council. It was the job of this Governing Council

Scouting is not soldiering

to assist the local committees and set policy for the Boy Scouts. Similar Boy Scout organizations were already being formed in several foreign countries.

By now, B-P realized that he could no longer do justice to both the Boy Scouts and the Army. He had hoped that scouting would give boys a new sense of purpose and direction, and that is exactly what the movement had given its founder. He felt that he should now devote all his time and energy to it.

In May, 1910, he submitted his application for retirement from the Army. At fifty-three, though much below the usual retirement age, he was granted a lieutenant-general's pension that would free him from any future financial worries. The famous soldier's military career had come to an end.

"It was a big wrench to take this last step out of the Service that I had loved so well," he wrote, "though at the same time I did not mind taking my foot off the ladder, for I had no wish to do any further climbing up it. I was not built for a General. I liked being regimental officer in touch with my men.

"It was no small consolation to receive from the Secretary of State for War a letter expressing his kindly regret in losing me from the Army, in which he added: '. . . But I feel that the organization of your Boy Scouts has so important a bearing on the future that probably the greatest service you can render to the country is to devote yourself to it.'

"And so ended my Life Number One."

15

An Important Journey

BADEN-POWELL HAD introduced scouting with British boys in mind, but the surprising thing, to many people, was that scouting appealed just as strongly to boys of other nationalities. By the time B-P retired from the Army, boys were taking the Scout Oath in fourteen nations outside the British Empire.

As the movement spread, B-P received many invitations to visit the new Boy Scout associations overseas. The first invitations he accepted came from Canada and the United States. In the summer of 1910, he accompanied two patrols of English Scouts on a goodwill tour of Canada. Afterwards, the boys went camping in the Canadian Rockies while B-P traveled south to New York.

Scouting had reached the United States as the result of a "Good Turn" performed by an English Boy Scout. In the autumn of 1909, a Chicago publisher named William Boyce was visiting London on business. One evening he lost his way in a heavy fog and stopped to ask a newsboy for directions. The boy offered to guide Boyce to his destination and then refused to accept a tip from the grateful publisher. "I'm a Boy Scout," he announced, "and we don't accept payment for any Good Turn we can do."

Boyce never learned the newsboy's name. But he wanted to

know more about this new organization, so the next day he visited Scout headquarters in London. When he returned to Chicago, his baggage included a trunkful of Scout pamphlets, copies of *Scouting for Boys,* and sample badges and uniforms. Early in 1910 he helped organize the Boy Scouts of America.

Several outstanding youth leaders worked together to bring scouting to American boys. Among them were Edgar Robinson, Senior Secretary of the Y.M.C.A. Committee on Boys' Work, Ernest Thompson Seton, founder of the Woodcraft Indians, and Dan Beard, founder of the Sons of Daniel Boone. Seton was elected the first Chief Scout of the Boy Scouts of America and Beard became the first National Scout Commissioner.

The American movement was only a few months old but was already flourishing when B-P visited the United States in 1910. During his brief stay in New York, he spoke at a dinner attended by three hundred prominent educators, youth leaders, and journalists. "Those who heard him," said one of the guests, "understood why the Boy Scout movement had succeeded. This timely visit of the creator of the modern Boy Scout gave a sharp impetus to our work in America."

In the following months, B-P visited Boy Scouts and their leaders in Belgium, Holland, Denmark, Norway, Sweden, and Russia. Then he was asked to return to the United States, this time for a cross-country lecture tour. He decided to extend the trip and go all the way around the world to inspect the new Scout associations in Japan, the Philippines, Australia, New Zealand, and South Africa.

It would prove to be the longest and most important journey he had ever taken.

Several hundred local Scouts were waiting at the pier in

Southampton to cheer the British Chief Scout when he boarded the S.S. *Arcadian* to begin his journey on the evening of January 3, 1912. B-P stopped to chat with the boys, then walked up the gangplank, waved goodbye, and sailed for the West Indies and New York.

After breakfast the next morning, he took a brisk walk on the ship's promenade deck. The *Arcadian* was ploughing through high seas and biting winter winds, and only a few other passengers were out on deck. Up ahead, B-P saw two young women. He recognized one as a family friend, Miss Hildabert Rodewald. He did not know her companion, yet there was something about the way the girl walked that seemed strangely familiar.

As he approached the women he took his hat off to greet them. "Why, General," Miss Rodewald said, "I had no idea you were aboard." Then she turned to her companion. "I want you to meet my good friend, Miss Olave Soames."

Olave Soames was a tall, elegant young lady with a quick smile, a direct manner, and inquiring brown eyes. B-P bowed gallantly. "Delighted," he said. He looked carefully at Miss Soames, then remembered where he had seen her.

"Don't you live in London?" he asked.

"No, in Dorset."

"But you have a brown and white spaniel, don't you?"

"Yes." Miss Soames was surprised.

"Weren't you ever in London? Near Knightsbridge Barracks?"

"Yes, two years ago."

Two years earlier, while B-P had been hurrying through Kensington Gardens on his way to Knightsbridge Barracks, he had noticed a young lady with a brown and white spaniel. Her quick, determined walk had intrigued him; it revealed, he wrote later, "honesty of purpose and common sense, as well as the spirit of adventure." They had not spoken. Indeed, their eyes had not met. But the image of the walking girl in the park had stayed with him.

Now he had met her.

Miss Soames was flattered that B-P remembered her after such a brief encounter, and she was thrilled to meet the famous General. She had been a ten-year-old girl during the siege of Mafeking and she remembered wearing on her dress a little button with B-P's portrait. As they talked, they discovered that they shared the same birthday, February 22. There was quite a difference in their ages, however. Olave Soames was twenty-two; Baden-Powell was fifty-four.

That evening at the captain's table, B-P was introduced to Miss Soames' father. Harold Soames was a wealthy retired businessman; with his daughter he was on his way to Jamaica for a winter holiday. He knew Baden-Powell by reputation and was anxious to chat with him.

The next morning, Olave Soames appeared on the promenade deck alone. B-P was waiting to join her. And in the following days, as the *Arcadian* steamed across the blustery Atlantic toward the warm sun of the Caribbean, they saw each other constantly.

B-P was amazed at himself. A shipboard romance had certainly not been part of his plans, yet he could not see enough of Olave. They talked and laughed together so easily, and they seemed to think and feel alike about so many things. When they were together, he wondered at his great good fortune in meeting her. When they were apart, he could not stop thinking about her.

For years he had put the Army first and had had little time for any personal life. The Army had always meant unexpected departures and long absences, uncertainty and danger. It was a difficult life for a family man, and like many other career soldiers, B-P had remained a bachelor. But he realized now that he had never married simply because he had never met anyone like Olave Soames.

Though she was much younger than he, his mother had been nearly thirty years younger than his father, and their marriage had been ideally happy. Only one thing seemed important: Olave would leave the ship with her father when they reached Jamaica, while B-P would have to continue his round-the-world journey without her.

Olave was having similar thoughts. Her letters home were dominated by "the only interesting person on board . . . the Scout man." And in the privacy of her diary, she began to call him her "beloved Scout."

When they went ashore at Kingston, Jamaica, B-P asked Olave to marry him and she accepted. Their first impulse was to have the Captain of the *Arcadian* perform a civil ceremony right away. But they both knew that this was impossible. Proper etiquette required a formal announcement and a church wedding, and since the wedding would have to wait until they both returned to England, they decided to keep their engagement a secret for the time being. Then B-P boarded the *Arcadian* again, and with a singing heart sailed north to New York.

For the next six months he was constantly on the move. He toured the United States, inspecting Scout troops, conferring with Scout leaders, and speaking before large audiences in New York, Boston, Washington, D.C., Pittsburgh, Detroit, Chicago, San Francisco, Portland, and Seattle. Then he sailed across the Pacific to visit Boy Scouts in Tokyo and Yokahama, in Shanghai and Hong Kong, and in Manila. He had his first look at the rapidly growing Scout movements in Australia and New Zealand, and he wound up his trip with a scouting tour of South Africa.

It was a strenuous and often hectic trip, filled with dinners and receptions, meetings and conferences, lectures and speeches. Yet B-P found great joy and satisfaction in this round-the-world journey. For wherever his ship docked, wherever his train stopped, crowds of Boy Scouts met him at the pier or station and later put on rousing rallies and demonstrations in his honor.

Scouting had traveled around the world ahead of its founder.

When Baden-Powell returned to England, he found himself cast in the traditional role of a nervous suitor. To begin with he had to visit Olave's home in Parkstone, Dorset, and ask Harold Soames for his daughter's hand in marriage. The very idea of this meeting made him so apprehensive that he cut himself shaving, missed his train, and arrived two hours late.

Afterwards, Olave came up to London to meet the Baden-Powell family. She had tea with B-P's elderly mother, his sister Agnes, and his brothers. Mrs. Baden-Powell was delighted. She had been urging B-P to marry for years.

Then B-P and Olave announced their engagement. While Scouts the world over rejoiced at this unexpected news, a few had misgivings. One boy wrote to Baden-Powell:

"I am dreadfully disappointed in you. I have often thought to myself 'How glad I am that the Chief Scout is not married, because if he was he could never do all these ripping things for boys.' And now you are going to do it. It is the last thing I should have expected of you. Of course, you won't be able to keep on with the Scouts the same as before, because your wife

B-P and Olave

will want you, and everything will fall through. I think it is awfully selfish of you."

B-P answered his young critic through one of his weekly columns in *The Scout* magazine: "I can assure the Scouts that the writer is wrong. I shall keep on with the Scouts just as much as ever. My future bride is as keen about Scouting as I am; she will help me in the work, so that my marriage instead of taking me from the movement will bring in another assistant to it, and one who loves the Scouts as they, I am sure, will love her so soon as they get to know her."

B-P's old army comrades wanted to assemble outside the church and cheer the newlyweds. Some Scout officials wanted a Boy Scout honor guard to surround the bride's home and line the road to the church. B-P and Olave wanted nothing of the sort. They discouraged these plans and agreed on a small, simple family ceremony.

They were married on October 30, 1912, at St. Peter's Church in Parkstone. Olave was given in marriage by her father. B-P's sister Agnes was maid of honor, and his younger brother Baden was best man. When the ceremony was over, the bells of St. Peter's rang out, the newlyweds ran through a shower of rice, climbed into a motor-car, waved goodbye, and drove off for their rented flat in London.

Since the wedding had been a private family affair, B-P and Olave invited several hundred relatives and friends to a wedding reception in London. One of the guests was General Louis Botha, who had fought against the British during the Boer War. Now Botha was the Prime Minister of South Africa, and was visiting London on government business. During the wedding reception he raised his glass and offered a toast to "the lady who has captured the man we could never catch."

On their honeymoon, B-P and Olave went camping in Algeria, "out on the desert, far from human habitation, in the glorious sunshine of North Africa." This was a new experience for Olave, but to B-P's delight she proved herself a first-class camper. "Olave is a perfect wonder in camp," he wrote to his mother. "She thoroughly enjoys the life. . . . You were so right, my dear Ma, when you said one ought to marry a young woman."

Back in England, B-P and Olave soon decided that they wanted to live outside London. And so they rented a spacious country house near the village of Robertsbridge, Sussex, within easy reach of the city. Their three children were born in this house—Peter in 1913 (on his parents' first wedding anniversary), Heather in 1915, and Betty in 1917.

16

Chief Scout of the World

As CHIEF SCOUT of Great Britain, B-P attended a great many camps, rallies and exhibitions all over the British Isles. The Imperial Scout Exhibition of 1913 was especially important. For a full week thousands of boys camped in a park outside Birmingham, England, while at a big exhibition hall in the city they demonstrated a wide variety of scouting skills.

Most of the boys came from Great Britain and her overseas dominions, colonies, and possessions. But this was more than just an Empire gathering, for the British Boy Scouts Association had also invited representative Scout patrols from a dozen foreign countries: Austria, Belgium, Denmark, France, Germany, Holland, Italy, Norway, Poland, Spain, Sweden, and the United States.

The Imperial Scout Exhibition was the first international gathering of Boy Scouts, and it was so successful that Scout leaders planned to hold similar events, with many more countries represented, in future years. B-P was greatly encouraged by this development. He believed more strongly than ever that the Scout movement could help hasten the day "of future peace among nations, when their men begin to look upon each other as members of one brotherhood instead of as hereditary enemies."

That day was yet to come, however, for within another year Europe had plunged into World War I. Some of the boys who had met in friendship at Birmingham the summer before, now found themselves shooting at each other.

Baden-Powell had called his movement "peace-scouting," and despite the war, scouting still aimed at the future ideal of world brotherhood. For the Scout Law said: "A Scout is a friend to all, and a brother to every other Scout, no matter to what country, class, or creed the other may belong."

But the Scout Law also said that a Scout is loyal to his country, and the Boy Scouts of many warring nations came to the aid of their countries in 1914. In England, the Boy Scout bugler, wearing his wide-brimmed hat and sounding the "All Clear" after an air raid, became a familiar wartime symbol. Under B-P's leadership, British Scouts helped guard bridges and telephone lines against sabotage; they worked as orderlies in hospitals, collected scrap, and went out into the fields to harvest crops. British Sea Scouts formed a special coast-guard force that patroled the nation's shoreline, freeing regular members of the Coast Guard for duty at sea.

B-P had offered his own services to the War Office; many officials there felt that he should be put in command of an army division. But Lord Kitchener, the Secretary of State for War, disagreed. He thought it was more important for Baden-Powell to continue his full-time job as a leader of the nation's youth. "I can find several competent divisional generals," Kitchener said, "but I know of no one who can carry on the invaluable work of the Boy Scouts."

B-P did make several trips to the battle zone in France,

where he visited troops on the front lines, toured hospitals, and helped set up several rear-area recreation centers financed by Boy Scout and Girl Guide contributions. But he devoted most of his time to scouting, suggesting new ways for British Scouts to aid the war effort and looking forward to the day when the movement could again become a force for peace.

During the war, the movement continued to expand. Younger boys had been clamoring to become Scouts for some time now. B-P felt that they needed a separate organization of their own, and in 1916 he wrote the *Wolf Cub's Handbook* for youngsters between the ages of nine and eleven. Scouting for girls was also growing rapidly, and in 1918 B-P completed a new handbook called *Girl Guiding,* which introduced a separate scouting program for younger girls, or Brownies.

Olave Baden-Powell, eager to work at her husband's side, played a key role in the growth of the girls' movement. In 1916 the Executive Committee of the Girl Guides asked her to take on the job of Chief Commissioner. And in 1918, Lady Baden-Powell was elected Chief Guide of Great Britain.

With the end of World War I, B-P wanted to plan a mass gathering of Boy Scouts from many nations. Some Scout leaders felt that the idea was too optimistic, too idealistic. They feared that an international Scout gathering, coming so soon after a bitter world conflict, could not possibly succeed. One man warned that if the ambitious plan was carried out, scouting might "totter to its fall."

"You take too serious a view of the whole matter," B-P replied. "If the movement is tottering, let it totter. As a matter of fact, it has plenty of vitality under the surface, and is quite capable of doing a very big thing in promoting international friendship—and what's more, it is going to do it."

Earlier scouting events had been called "rallies," "exhibitions" or "displays," but B-P considered these words much too ordinary to describe the first post-war meeting of the world's Scouts. On a visit to the United States he had heard a new word—"jamboree." Now he suggested that the forthcoming gathering be called the Boy Scout International Jamboree.

Again, he met with objections. A few Scout officials complained that this American slang expression was not at all suited to an important scouting event. The dictionary defined "jamboree" as "a noisy revel; a carousal or spree." B-P argued that boys, after all, were rather noisy when they got together, and that one of the main ideas of the international gathering was for everyone to make friends and have a good time. So why not Jamboree?

No one could come up with a better term, and after saying "jamboree" to each other a few times, the critical Scout leaders began to like the sound of the word. Today, most dictionaries define "jamboree" as both a "noisy revel" and as "a rally of Boy Scouts."

Yet no single word can really capture the spirit and excitement of that first Jamboree, held in 1920 at Olympia, an enormous glass-roofed exhibition hall in London. Boy Scouts, Sea Scouts, Senior Scouts, and Cub Scouts converged on London from every part of the British Empire and from twenty-one foreign countries. Holland sent the largest foreign delegation—four hundred boys. Japan sent the smallest—two boys. The United States contingent of three hundred Scouts represented every state in the Union. Other delegations came from Belgium, Chile, China, Denmark, Estonia, France, Greece, Italy, Luxembourg, Norway, Poland, Portugal, Rumania, Serbia, Siam, Spain, Sweden, and Switzerland. And there were separate British Empire contingents from Scotland, Wales,

THE BOY SCOUTS'
INTERNATIONAL JAMBOREE

OLYMPIA,

July 30th to August 7th, 1920.

▭

FEATURES OF THE JAMBOREE WILL BE :—

Demonstrations of Scouting and Woodcraft Activities.

International Competitions for the World's Scout
Championships.

Scout Handicrafts Exhibition.   Boy Scout Zoo.

Grand Displays twice daily in the Arena.

*Program for the first Boy Scouts' International Jamboree,
London, 1920*

Ireland, Australia, New Zealand, Malaya, India, Ceylon, South Africa, the West Indies, and Malta.

The Jamboree opened on July 30 and for the next nine days spectators thronged to Olympia by the tens of thousands as the Scouts of the world put on a dazzling series of rallies, exhibitions, displays, and competitions. Scout bands played, Scout choirs chorused, and Scout buglers bugled. Boys tumbled, wrestled and raced; they pitched tents, laid fires, built huts and bridges, and sent signals; they exhibited Scout handicrafts and displayed working models of airplanes, steam engines, automobiles, electric toys, and watermills; they took part in first-aid, life-saving, fire-fighting, and pathfinding demonstrations, tug-of-war contests, obstacle races, and in a marathon bicycle ride through one hundred miles of open country outside London. The tracking strip was especially popular; here spectators and Scouts alike crowded around to talk and argue about the different set of clues and tracks laid out every day.

Each delegation presented is own show. Swedish Scouts demonstrated Swedish gymnastics, Jamaican Scouts depicted the tribal customs of the Arawak Indians, and Dutch Scouts performed their national wooden shoe dance. The American delegation, which included several boys of Indian descent, presented a colorful "American Indian Pageant," featuring feathered head-dresses, teepees, live ponies, war-dances, and a peace-pipe ceremony to which Baden-Powell was invited. At the end of the ceremony, the boys placed an Indian bonnet on B-P's head and proclaimed him "Chief Lone Pine on the Skyline."

Scouts taking part in the daily exhibits stayed at Olympia during the Jamboree. Thousands of other Scouts camped at Old Deer Park on the outskirts of London. Wherever the boys stayed, they had plenty of opportunity to mingle and make

Scouts of many nations at the first Jamboree

friends, and though they spoke two dozen different languages, they quickly worked out their own means of communication called "Jamboreese." There were Scouts of every color at this Jamboree, Scouts of many religions and widely differing backgrounds, yet they were all united by the same Scout Law and linked by a common bond of shared interests and ideals.

Public reaction to the Jamboree was expressed by a *Punch* magazine cartoon which depicted the "War-weary World" greeting a group of Scouts from different countries and saying: "I was nearly losing hope, but the sight of all you boys gives it back to me."

Baden-Powell had never completely overcome his surprise at the immense world-wide appeal of scouting, and now he took obvious delight in this first Jamboree. He was seen everywhere —touring the displays and exhibits at Olympia, taking part in pageants and other special events, visiting the camp at Old Deer Park, chatting with the boys in their tents, joining them at meals, posing for snapshots, telling stories at evening campfires.

Many boys were understandably nervous when B-P came around for the first time. He was a famous man, after all—Sir Robert Baden-Powell, the Founder of their movement—and most Scouts had seen him before only as a distant figure at rallies. But B-P knew how to put a fellow Scout at ease. He never spoke *to* a boy; he chatted *with* him, asking about the boy's interests and ambitions, and exchanging ideas with him on a man-to-man basis.

As the Jamboree continued, some of the boys got together with their leaders and discussed paying a special tribute to Baden-Powell. This tribute was planned without his knowledge and was secretly scheduled for the closing evening of the Jamboree, on Saturday, August 7.

A capacity audience packed the big exhibition hall that evening as the program started off with the final competitions for the international Scout championships; Denmark won both the trek-cart obstacle race championship and the tug-of-war championship. British Scouts put on a camping display. American Scouts gave a repeat performance of their popular Indian Pageant.

The program ended with a colorful ceremony symbolizing international friendship. A girl dressed as Britannia entered at one end of the exhibition hall, followed by all the Scouts from Great Britain. Another girl, dressed as Columbia, appeared at the opposite end of the hall, followed by Scouts from the United States. Britannia and Columbia approached each other in the central arena and embraced. Then they mounted a dais as the British and American Scouts assembled around them.

Now from outside the hall came the distant sounds of music and tramping feet. The sounds drew nearer, and nearer still, and then the Scouts of the world began to march into the arena by the thousands. Each contingent was led by two standard-bearers holding aloft their country's flag and the green banner of the Scouts. Many of the boys were wearing their national costumes.

When all the Scouts had entered the vast arena, the stand-ard-bearers left their contingents, moved forward, and formed an imposing avenue of flags leading from the central dais to the Royal Box at one side of the hall, where B-P was sitting with Lady Baden-Powell and the Chief Scouts of all countries represented at the Jamboree. Britannia and Columbia left their places on the dais and approached the Royal Box. B-P rose to greet them and they accompanied him back to the dais beneath an arch of flags. As he passed by, the flag of each nation was dipped in his honor. He mounted the dais alone and turned to face the crowd, ready to deliver his closing ad-dress.

To this point, the ceremony had been carefully rehearsed. What happened next came as a complete surprise to B-P and to the audience of fifteen thousand spectators.

Before he could start speaking, a boy's voice rang out through the hall: "We, the Scouts of the World, salute you, Sir Robert Baden-Powell—Chief Scout of the World!"

The Scouts began to cheer, and again the standard-bearers dipped their flags in B-P's honor. He hesitated, his face flushed. Until now he had been simply Chief Scout of Great Britain; each nation had its own Chief Scout. By proclaiming him Chief Scout of the World, the boys had granted him an honor only they could confer.

For a few moments, B-P gazed silently at the cheering boys massed before him. Then he raised his hand in the Scout sign, and the cheers subsided. He was a man of sixty-three now, but his voice was still remarkably young and strong:

"Brother Scouts, I ask you to make a solemn choice. Differences exist between peoples of the world in thought and temperament, just as they do in language and physique. The War has taught us that when one nation tries to impose its particular will upon others, cruel reaction is bound to follow. The Jamboree has taught us that if we exercise mutual forebearance and give and take, then there is sympathy and harmony.

"If it be your will, let us go forth from here fully determined that we will develop among ourselves that comradeship, through the world-wide spirit of Scout Brotherhood, which may help us develop peace and happiness in the world and good will among men.

"Brother Scouts, answer me. Will you join me in this endeavor?"

The Scouts answered with a resounding "Yes!"

"God speed you in your work," B-P replied, "and fare you well."

A bugler sounded the Last Post. Boys and men throughout the hall came to the Scout salute and the audience rose as a laurel wreath was raised on the flagpole at the far end of the arena, in memory of all Scouts who had died during World War I.

Then the American Scout band struck up "Auld Lang Syne" and boys of the British and American contingents linked arms and began singing. Though the words were unfamiliar to many of the other boys, they quickly caught on. "Seeing what their brother Scouts were doing," *The Scouter* magazine reported, "and realizing that it was good, the Malay boys took up the chain. From them it ran quickly to the Scouts from Jamaica, and spread to all the boys in the arena. Not stopping there, it passed on to the audience. Everywhere arms were linked as the sentiment of the song spread to every corner of the building."

In the entire exhibition hall, there was only one lonely figure. The Chief Scout of the World stood by himself in the center of the arena, looking first one way, then the other, surrounded by singing boys. Suddenly he dived into the front rank of the American contingent. Two Scouts stepped apart to admit their Chief. Then they closed ranks again, linking their arms with his.

When the singing ended, the Scouts again broke into cheers and began to fling their hats into the air. B-P returned to the Royal Box to watch the boys file out of the hall. But they were not yet willing to leave, for now Scouts and spectators alike were being swept up in a wild, spontaneous demonstration. The band was blaring. Flags were weaving back and forth. Scout hats danced and flickered in the air. And the cheering grew louder and louder, swelling and reverberating until it seemed that the gigantic glass roof of the exhibition hall must surely quiver and shatter.

Finally, one of the boys was sent up to the Royal Box to tell B-P that he must return to the arena. Otherwise, the Scouts would fetch him.

"The Chief returned," reported *The Scouter,* "but in a moment he was swallowed up in a sea of excited boyhood. He disappeared from view. Then he reappeared, perched on the shoulders of some strong fellows in the center of the throng.

"Slowly he was borne nearer to the side of the arena. One supreme effort and he was free to climb up the tiers of seats until he could again reach the Royal Box. In the arena it was still pandemonium. A roar as of thunder filled the whole building, but on a single bugle note it at once subsided.

"The Jamboree was over."

On Monday morning, the London *Times* commented: "At the close of the great Jamboree at Olympia on Saturday night, Boy Scouts acclaimed Sir Robert Baden-Powell as Chief Scout of the World. Well did he deserve it, for through him a great gift has come to the boys of Great Britain, and from them has spread to the boys of all nations."

17

The Spirit of Scout Brotherhood

THE SCOUT MOVEMENT had started in 1907 with twenty-one English boys carrying out an experiment on Brownsea Island. When the first world Scout census was taken in 1922, there were more than one million Boy Scouts in thirty-two countries.

The steady growth of the movement had encouraged Scout leaders to establish an International Committee and Bureau, with headquarters in London. In the first issue of the Bureau's magazine, *Jamboree,* Baden-Powell spelled out the aims of world scouting:

"We have seen with our own eyes the international development of our Brotherhood and we have realized that the true spirit of Scout comradeship inspires it, a spirit which recognizes no difference of country, creed, color, or class. . . . While we are building up, each for the good of our country, our own individual associations of Boy Scouts and Girl Guides as a school of young citizens, let us keep ever before us the still greater aim of promoting comradeship with our brother Scouts in other lands."

Although each country came to interpret scouting in its own way, B-P was constantly being called upon for his advice and leadership. During the 1920's and 1930's, he and Lady Baden-Powell traveled widely, visiting virtually every country on earth that had a scouting movement. They attended Boy Scout Jamborees and Girl Guide World Camps on five continents. Twice they sailed around the world, meeting Scouts and Guides in such out-of-the-way places as Sierra Leone, St. Helena, Ceylon, Burma, Malaya, Madeira, Tahiti, and Iceland.

At British Empire scouting events, B-P often met the sons and grandsons of men he had known in the 13th Hussars, the 5th Dragoon Guards, and the South African Constabulary, and of men who had fought with him and against him in Ashanti, in Matabeleland, and at Mafeking. He was especially pleased when a delegation of African Scouts from the Gold Coast and Ashanti attended the Wembley Empire Jamboree in London in 1924. While he had never had a chance to return to Ashanti, he was still remembered there. The African boys greeted him by his old nickname, "Kantankye"—"He of the Big Hat"—and put on a demonstration of Ashanti "drum-talk." Some of the boys had brought personal messages from their fathers, warriors and scouts who had marched with B-P on the road to Kumasi in 1896.

The Boy Scouts of America invited B-P back to the United States in 1926 to present him with their first Silver Buffalo, a new award "for distinguished service to boyhood." As Silver

Buffalo Number One was hung around the Chief's neck on its red-and-white silk ribbon, he was told that Silver Buffalo Number Two was being awarded to the English newsboy who once guided publisher William Boyce through a London fog—sending Boyce back home determined to start an American branch of scouting. Since the newsboy was still unknown, a statue of a buffalo was erected in Gilwell Park, the international Scoutmasters' training center near London. The inscription on the statue reads:

To the Unknown Scout Whose Faithfulness in the
Performance of the Daily Good Turn Brought the
Scout Movement to the United States of America

After the first Jamboree in England, Scout leaders had decided to plan similar events in different countries every four years. The Second International Jamboree was held near Copenhagen, Denmark, in 1924. "Scouting gives a wider outlook of a brotherland beyond the borders of the Motherland," B-P told the assembled Scouts from thirty-three nations. "It has opened the eyes of all of us to the fact that boys are alike the world over. They are by nature free from the prejudices and suspicions of their fathers."

The third Jamboree should have taken place in 1928, in some country other than England or Denmark. However Scout leaders agreed to delay this gathering until 1929, the twenty-first anniversary of scouting, and to hold it again in England, where the movement was born. Called the Coming-of-Age Jamboree, it was the most ambitious scouting event up to that time. Some thirty thousand boys came to Birkenhead, England, from thirty-one parts of the British Empire and from forty-one foreign countries.

To help celebrate scouting's twenty-first birthday, King George V of England wanted to confer a peerage on the Chief Scout. The King's father, Edward VII, had knighted Baden-Powell years earlier and had made him a baronet. George V now wanted to elevate B-P to the higher rank of baron, making him a peer, or nobleman. He would then become Lord Baden-Powell.

B-P did not wish to be a lord, however, and he insisted that he would refuse the peerage. He regarded it as too much a personal honor, and as Chief Scout of the World, felt it would be inappropriate for him to accept. Other Scout leaders disagreed. They argued that a peerage granted to the Chief Scout would be a tribute to the entire movement, and they finally persuaded B-P to change his mind.

A peer's name is customarily followed by a territorial designation, and B-P had the right to select his own title. Some people suggested that he become Lord Baden-Powell of Mafeking. He rejected this idea because Mafeking symbolized his army life; he wanted his title to be associated clearly with world scouting. Since Gilwell Park near London was the permanent training center for Scout leaders from all over the world, he decided to become Lord Baden-Powell of Gilwell.

Although B-P was now in his seventies, scouting had kept him young, and he rejoiced in his visits to Scout jamborees, rallies, and camps all over the world. A reporter from the *Sydney Morning Herald* has left us a vivid glimpse of the Chief Scout during his visit to a Jamboree in Australia in 1931:

"With an agility that would put to shame many men half his age, Lord Baden-Powell descended steep tracks, clambered up rocks, walked along paths above which rain-wet scrub hung heavily. With the eye of a pioneer he looked appraisingly at camps and fireplaces. . . . The sun was setting as he arrived.

The Chief Scout tests a bridge

As he went from one to the other of the forty-eight different campsites, here and there fires glinted through the gathering gloom, blue smoke curled into the still air. And the smell of frying sausages was wafted through the bush. Billies of boiling water bubbled merrily. Smiling boyish faces shone in the flickering light of fires.

"It was all delightfully informal. Many of the Scouts seemed unaware that the Big Chief was among them. 'Hey, Jack, I dodged you!' yelled one youngster from the top of a rock to a mate who chased him. They did not see the keen-eyed Big Chief watching them from a path above them. 'Hey, Jacky, you can't cat . . .' Suddenly he saw Lord Baden-Powell— stopped in the middle of a word, and came as nearly to attention as he could on his precarious perch.

"In the center of a large cleared space stood a heap of firewood. Baden-Powell was asked to light it—around it, later in the evening, was to be a 'wood badge' investiture. Now no Scout must use more than two matches in lighting a fire. B-P took several and in the end had to invoke the aid of a *Herald* representative's copy-paper. At that moment the Chief Guide appeared.

" 'I took more than two matches,' said B-P shamefacedly.

" 'Awful!' replied the Chief Guide, and B-P, true Scout that he is, did not excuse himself by saying, as he could have said, that the laying of the fire was not his doing, nor did he blame the dampness of the wood."

When Baden-Powell introduced scouting in England, he insisted that the movement welcome boys of every class and creed. As scouting spread overseas, he insisted with equal conviction that it must also welcome boys of every nationality and race. Yet it was not always easy to put the ideal of Scout brotherhood into practice.

While B-P had no actual control over Scout associations outside Great Britain, he did have considerable influence, and he did not hesitate to speak out. He was particularly concerned with prejudice in India and South Africa, where he had spent so many years of his life.

India was still a British colony, and scouting there had been restricted at first to boys of British parentage. Government officials had forbidden Indian boys to join the recognized Boy Scouts Association. Despite these officials, scouting appealed to Indian boys just as it appealed to boys everywhere, and several unrecognized Scout associations sprang up in the various states and provinces of India.

In one of their first trips after World War I, B-P and Lady Baden-Powell went to India hoping to bring all British and Indian Scouts there together within the same organization. "I am sailing today for India on a mission which I hope . . . is one you will approve," B-P wrote to an Indian friend. "I do not know to what extent you may have studied the ideals and progress of the Boy Scout Movement. . . . It has overrun the borders of country, class and creed, and is already establishing itself as a brotherhood among the young in every nation, on the basis of their common membership in the human family."

For several weeks the Baden-Powells toured the country, meeting with government officials and with leaders of the British Boy Scouts Association, the Indian Boy Scouts Association, and other Scout groups. B-P finally persuaded everyone concerned to attend a conference in the city of Madras. This conference was a complete success, for it resulted in an agreement to form a single, unified Scout association for all boys living in India.

"We who had sat down to the talk as a meeting of representative heads," reported the pleased Chief Scout, "rose at the end of it a united band of brother Scouts."

South Africa presented more difficult problems, for racial barriers there were deeply entrenched and stubbornly upheld. Officially recognized scouting was confined to boys of British and Dutch descent. African boys had started their own unofficial organization, the Pathfinder Scouts. Other unofficial Scout groups had been formed by "Colored" boys of mixed European and African descent, and by boys of Indian descent.

South Africa had been the scene of Baden-Powell's greatest military adventures and triumphs. When he returned there during the 1920's and 1930's, however, he went not as an army officer pledged to defend the British Empire, but as the Chief Scout of the World, dedicated to the ideals of brotherhood. And in this land he had come to love, it grieved him that scouting should be divided along racial lines. He hoped to bring boys of all races together within a single Scout organization, similar to the one formed in India.

This goal was never realized. After several visits to South Africa, after innumerable meetings and conferences with government officials and Scout leaders there, the best B-P could achieve was a compromise. In 1936 the South Africa Scout Council agreed to recognize four parallel Scout organizations: the Boy Scouts Association of the Union for white boys, Pathfinder Boy Scouts for African boys, Colored Boy Scouts, and Indian Boy Scouts. While each organization would observe the same scouting principles, each would continue to be run along racial lines.

B-P was not satisfied with this compromise, but he had to accept it as the best arrangement possible in South Africa at that time. "Our policy of making the Movement open to all, regardless of class, creed or color, is still not put into full practice," he wrote. "One has to admit that this is so, but a real advance towards the ideal has been made, and with that one must at present remain content."

He still believed that Scouts in South Africa and everywhere would someday overcome the prejudices and suspicions of their fathers.

Early in their marriage, B-P and Olave lived in the rented

country home near Robertsbridge, Sussex, where their three children were born. When World War I ended, they bought a house of their own near the village of Bentley, Hampshire, not far from London. Since they found this house during the first days of peace after the Armistice, and since it stood high on a hill overlooking the beautiful Hampshire countryside, they called it "Pax Hill."

Pax Hill was their home for nearly twenty years—from 1919 to 1938. It was also the informal headquarters of world scouting. One of the many visitors to Pax Hill during these years was E.E. Reynolds, a British Scout leader and author of *Baden-Powell*. "No one who experienced the hospitality at Pax Hill," he wrote, "can ever forget the cheerfulness and happiness of the home life [B-P] and Lady Baden-Powell had together created. An unending stream of visitors passed through— distinguished men and women, old friends, leaders in the Scout and Guide worlds, Scouters and Guiders in need of a rest; and, in the summer, campers pitched their tents and came to know their friendly hosts. There was no ostentation or ceremony, but a warm-hearted welcome for all."

Although B-P was constantly busy at Pax Hill, he had learned to organize his time and he seemed always to have leisure for his family and friends. One of his secrets was his custom of rising early, a habit he had developed in India, where it was necessary to accomplish as much as possible before the mid-day heat set in. At Pax Hill he kept to the same schedule. He usually rose at 5 A.M., brewed himself a pot of tea, and settled down in his study while the house was still quiet, when he could concentrate without the interruptions of phone calls or visitors. By the time most people were having breakfast, he had already completed two or three hours work.

Around 7:30 or 8:00, he and Olave would go off on a coun-

B-P and his family at Pax Hill

try walk with their two Labrador retrievers. Afterwards the whole family would breakfast together, along with any guests staying at Pax Hill. Then B-P would return to his study, and with the help of his secretary, Mrs. A.G. Wade, he would start answering the morning mail. When the mail was out of the way, there were always reports to read, new scouting events to plan, meetings to attend in London, and articles to write for *The Scout, The Scouter,* and a variety of other magazines.

In addition to his many magazine columns and articles, B-P was usually working on a new book. Some of his books were collections of stories and advice for Boy Scouts and Girl Guides. Others concerned the Scout movement or described his personal travels and adventures. During a voyage around the world in 1933 he wrote his autobiography, *Lessons from the Varsity of Life.* This book, more than any other, perhaps, expresses the idealism, charm, and wit that made B-P such a stimulating and entertaining companion. He wrote more than thirty books in all.

Despite his heavy work schedule, he usually found time during the afternoon to sketch or paint, or to work in his garden. He also spent a great deal of time with his children. Since he had never enjoyed the companionship of a father, he knew how important this was.

There was plenty of space at Pax Hill for the menagerie of dogs, cats, rabbits, pigeons, and other pets that Peter, Heather, and Betty collected. Each child also had a pony to train and care for, and since their father was an old cavalryman, they all became expert riders. On summer holidays, the entire family often spent two or three weeks camping in the south of England, and sometimes B-P and Peter went off by themselves on fishing trips. When the children were old enough, they began to accompany their parents on scouting tours all over the world.

During these years, B-P described himself as an "intensely happy man." He was especially happy when the International Committee of the Girl Guides, in 1930, unanimously elected Lady Baden-Powell Chief Guide of the World.

"My wife," B-P said proudly, "has been my right hand in bringing up, not only our own children, but the vast family of Boy Scouts and Girl Guides."

18

I Have Gone Home

ROBERT BADEN-POWELL celebrated his eightieth birthday in 1937. He started the year by sailing to India with his wife and their daughter Heather. The Chief Scout and Chief Guide were to be guests of honor at the All-India Jamboree in New Delhi.

This was B-P's first visit to India since 1921, when he had unified the various Indian Scout organizations. Now he wanted to see for himself how scouting had fared there.

Scouts had come to New Delhi from every part of the Indian sub-continent. "The usual differences between provinces, races, religious castes, and classes were forgotten in the general spirit of brotherhood which pervaded the camp," B-P wrote. "All cooperated to show the public what scouting means, rather than to prove one lot as superior to another. Wild Baluchis met quieter Bengalis, the Nagas (sons of the head-hunters of Assam) chummed up with the boys of Bombay, the Pathans of the Punjab with the Burmese. It was a wonderfully mixed pudding. . . . an undoubted success from every point of view."

After the Jamboree B-P traveled to Risalpur on India's northwest frontier, where the 13th Hussars were stationed. He spent his eightieth birthday with his old regiment, reminiscing about those long ago days when he and Tommy Dimond had

The Chief Scout at eighty

joined the 13th as eager young subalterns. Once again he wore his full-dress uniform and watched the Hussars ride past in review, their horses prancing and snorting, the regimental colors flapping in the breeze, "I felt forty years younger on the spot," he said. "It was for me my last mounted parade."

The Baden-Powells sailed back to England in time to attend the coronation of King George VI in May, 1937. When the Coronation Honors were announced, B-P learned that he would receive the Order of Merit, held by only twenty-four other living persons. That same year the President of France conferred the Grand Cordon of the Legion of Honor upon him. And from the United States came word that the Carnegie Institute had awarded him its Wateler Peace Prize "for his services to World Peace and for promoting international good will through the Scout movement."

The Fifth World Jamboree was held that summer at Vogelenzang, Holland. While B-P had attended many impressive scouting events over the years, this one had a profound personal meaning for him. He was an old man now, and he felt that this would be his last Jamboree.

He was clearly moved by the Farewell March Past. It began at 2:30 P.M. in brilliant sunshine, and for nearly two hours boys from every continent paraded onto the field and swung past the reviewing stand to salute their Chief. Many of the boys shouted a greeting at B-P as they passed. Others cheered or waved. Overhead a giant dirigible circled the field. Aboard were handicapped Scouts; since they could not take part in the March Past, they had been invited to watch from the air.

When the last Scout had passed the reviewing stand, B-P mounted the speaker's platform, looked out over the gathering of some thirty thousand boys, and then spoke:

"We have come to the end of our Jamboree. It seems as if we were only beginning it yesterday and now we are already at the end. But during these few short days, I am very glad that all of you Scouts gathered from all parts of the world have been making the most of your opportunities to make friends. After all, that was the main object of the Jamboree, to make with those boys of countries other than your own as many friends as possible.

"We have been called a boys' Crusade, the Crusade of Peace, and it is a very apt description of our Brotherhood. . . .

"Now the time has come for me to say goodbye. I want you to lead happy lives. You know that many of us will never meet

*The Chief Scout with Queen Wilhelmina at the
Fifth World Jamboree, Vogelenzang, Holland*

again in this world. I am in my eighty-first year and am near-
ing the end of my life. Most of you are at the beginning and I
want your lives to be happy and successful. You can make them
so by doing your best to carry out the Scout Law all your days,
whatever your station and wherever you are. . . .

"Now goodbye. God bless you all."

Three months later, B-P and Olave celebrated their twenty-
fifth wedding anniversary at Pax Hill. Then they sailed for
Kenya in East Africa, where they planned to spend the
Christmas holidays with Eric Walker, an old friend who had
built a unique hotel called The Outspan at the town of Nyeri.
The Outspan's guest lived in small cottages set amidst tropical

gardens and spectacular mountain scenery, with the snow-capped peak of Mount Kenya visible forty miles away. B-P and Olave had visited The Outspan once before and had always wanted to return.

During their voyage south they stopped at several ports-of-call to attend Scout and Guide rallies. From Kenya they had expected to continue to South Africa. By the time they reached Nyeri, however, B-P was suffering from persistent headaches and a severe cough. He insisted that he simply needed a few days' rest, but when he failed to improve, Olave called in a doctor.

The Chief Scout spent New Year's Day of 1938 undergoing a medical examination. When the doctor asked him to describe his activities during the past year, B-P mentioned his voyage to India, the All-India Jamboree, his reunion with the 13th Hussars, his participation in the Coronation, the Fifth World Jamboree, the parties in honor of his wedding anniversary, and the Scout rallies he had attended while sailing to Kenya.

"Is that all?" the doctor asked. B-P nodded.

The doctor shook his head. "You're nearly eighty-one years old," he said. "If you haven't learned any sense by now, you deserve all the ills that have fallen upon you."

B-P was physically exhausted. The doctor told him that he needed a complete rest, that he should stop working for a year at least. His planned scouting tour of South Africa would have to be canceled.

It wasn't easy for the Chief Scout to accept this advice, but he knew that in the future he would have to play a less active role in the Scout movement.

Ever since their first visit to Nyeri, B-P and Olave had talked about building a small winter home at The Outspan.

This seemed an especially good idea now that two of their children were married and living in Africa. Peter and his wife, Carine, had settled in Southern Rhodesia and had presented B-P with his first grandchild and namesake, Robert. Betty was living in Northern Rhodesia with her husband, Gervas Clay; they had two children, Gillian and Robin Baden.

B-P and Olave discussed their plans for a winter home with Eric Walker, owner of The Outspan. He offered to make all the arrangements and promised that their cottage would be ready that autumn.

When B-P felt well enough to travel again, he and Olave sailed back to England where they spent most of the summer at Pax Hill. In August, they accompanied five hundred Scout and Guide leaders on a goodwill cruise to Belgium, Denmark, Norway, and Iceland. At each port of call B-P stood at the railing and waved to the Scouts and Guides who had come to greet him. But his doctors would not permit him to leave the ship.

Then he and Olave returned to Nyeri where their bungalow was waiting. It was a delightful little place with a big verandah, a garden of tropical flowers and trees, and a superb view of Mount Kenya. It would be their second home—a smaller Pax Hill, a Pax too, or a Pax Number Two. They called it "Paxtu"—a Swahili word meaning "complete."

B-P had been ordered to rest, but he had been active all his life and he could not really be idle now. He continued to write his regular columns for *The Scout* and *The Scouter* magazines, and he corresponded with scores of old friends the world over. He sketched and painted, worked in his tropical garden, and saw a great deal of the splendid countryside around Nyeri.

With friends, he and Olave would drive out to a nearby

game preserve and watch elephants, rhinos, giraffes, zebras, gazelles, and other wild animals in their natural settings. As a soldier, B-P had often gone big-game hunting. Since founding the Scout movement, however, he had given up hunting with a gun, for scouting taught a respect for all life and for the right of every creature to live. Now he stalked wild animals only with his camera.

"Where hunters used to compare notes over their rifles," he wrote, "they now do so with no less interest over their cameras. It implies more crafty stalking and as great daring and skill as ever. The trophies, especially if gained with a movie camera, form a far more exciting record both for yourself and for your friends than any dead horns and hides."

In 1939 B-P was nominated for the Nobel Peace Prize in recognition of his efforts to promote peace and friendship among nations through the Scout movement. But no Peace Prize was awarded that year. Before the Nobel Committee could meet, Hitler marched into Poland and World War II began.

B-P wanted to return to England, but his doctor would not permit it. "I have been pruning roses in my garden here in Kenya," he wrote home to British Scout leaders. "Not a very high-class job of service in wartime! I am not proud of it, but it is all that I am allowed of outdoor exercise, by my doctor."

His son Peter and son-in-law Gervas were both in government service. Early in 1940 they obtained leaves at the same time and brought their families to Nyeri. And for a few carefree days the war was forgotten as B-P and Olave enjoyed a happy reunion with their children and grandchildren. Only Heather was missing; she was serving with the women's branch of the Army in England. Heather had recently become engaged, and that summer she married John King. "It is good to feel," B-P told Olave, "that our youngsters are all happily married and established in life."

His own life, he knew, was approaching its end, for as the summer passed he felt increasingly weak. In September he became seriously ill and the doctor warned Olave that he might not live out the year. Yet the patient rallied. After a week he was able to walk in his garden again. Now he wrote farewell messages to Boy Scouts, Girl Guides, Scout and Guide leaders, and the general public.

In his message to Boy Scouts he said:

Dear Scouts—If you have ever seen the play *Peter Pan,* you will remember how the pirate chief was always making his dying speech, because he was afraid that possibly, when the time came for him to die, he might not have time to get it off his chest.

It is much the same with me; and so, although I am not at this moment dying, I shall be doing so one of these days, and I want to send you a parting word of goodbye.

Remember it is the last you will ever hear from me, so think it over.

I have had a most happy life, and I want each one of you to have as happy a life too.

I believe that God put us in this jolly world to be happy and enjoy life.

Happiness doesn't come from being rich, nor merely from being successful in your career, nor by self-indulgence.

One step towards happiness is to make yourself healthy and strong while you are a boy, so that you can *be useful,* and so can enjoy life when you are a man.

Nature study will show you how full of beautiful and wonderful things God has made the world for you to enjoy.

Be contented with what you have got, and make the best of it; look on the bright side of things instead of the gloomy one. But the real way to get happiness is by giving out happiness to other people.

Try and leave this world a little better than you found it, and when your turn comes to die you can die happy in feeling that at any rate you have not wasted your time but have *done your best*.

'Be Prepared' in this way, to live happy and die happy; stick to your Scout Promise always—even after you have ceased to be a boy—and God help you to do it.

Your friend,
Baden-Powell

As the year drew to a close, B-P's strength gradually ebbed. He was confined to bed now, drifting in and out of sleep, dreaming perhaps of another time, another century, when he and his brothers had raced laughing and shouting across fragrant English meadows under a golden summer sun.

Olave sat by his bedside, and he held her hand tightly. On January 7, 1941, he lapsed into unconsciousness. At 5:45 on the morning of January 8, Robert Baden-Powell died.

He had asked to be buried in Africa, and the funeral paid tribute to both his lives. Soldiers and Scouts, black and white, escorted the Chief to his last resting place in the tiny cemetery at Nyeri, Kenya. His grave is marked by a simple stone engraved with his name and with the Boy Scout trail sign meaning, "I have gone home."

"I have gone home"—Nyeri, Kenya, 1941

Robert Baden-Powell had dreamed of "a brotherhood among the young in every nation, on the basis of their common membership in the human family." Today, in nearly one hundred countries, ten million active Boy Scouts and six million active Girl Guides and Girl Scouts are doing their best to bring about just such a brotherhood.

May Your
Happiest Dreams
come true!

Baden Powell

Bibliographical Note

Much of the research for this book was done at Baden-Powell House, the Scouts' international center in London. A permanent exhibition there, *The Baden-Powell Story,* presents through a dramatic sequence of words, sound and pictures the highlights of B-P's life and includes many key documents, momentoes, and photographs. The library at Baden-Powell House contains an extensive collection of books, periodicals, and other materials dealing with the Scout movement and its founder. I am particularly grateful to the staff for permitting me to see some old family scrapbooks, clippings, and other personal effects not on exhibit or available in the library.

Baden-Powell's own writings—his books, articles, pamphlets and speeches—were among my chief sources. I have quoted directly from the first edition of *Scouting for Boys* and from the following autobiographical works: *Lessons from the Varsity of Life, Indian Memories, My Adventures as a Spy, Adventures and Accidents, The Downfall of Prempeh, The Matabele Campaign, Sketches in Mafeking and East Africa, An Old Wolf's Favorites,* and *Yarns for Boy Scouts.* I have also quoted from back issues of *The Scout, The Scouter,* and

Jamboree and from some of the earlier Jamboree logbooks.

In addition to the above sources, I am indebted to the authoritative biography *Baden-Powell: The Two Lives of a Hero* by William Hillcourt with Olave, Lady Baden-Powell (New York: Putnam's, 1964), and to two excellent books by E.E. Reynolds, *Baden-Powell* (New York: Oxford, 1943) and *The Scout Movement* (London: Oxford, 1950). Other books which proved especially helpful include *B-P's Scouts: The Official History of the Boy Scouts Association* by Henry Collis, Fred Hurll, and Rex Hazlewood (London: Collins, 1961); *Twenty-Seven Years with Baden-Powell* by E.K. Wade (London: Blandford, 1957); *Mafeking: A Diary of the Siege* by F.D. Baillie (Westminster: Constable, 1900); and *Baden-Powell at Mafeking* by Duncan Grinnell-Milne (London: Bodley Head, 1957).

Finally, I wish to thank Mr. Paul Tabori of London for his first-hand account of Baden-Powell and the Scout movement during the 1930's.

RUSSELL FREEDMAN

Index

219